Gil G. Noam
Editor-in-Chief

NEW DIRECTIO

YOUTH DEVELO

ory

ctice

search

winter   2006

Rethinking Programs
for Youth in the
Middle Years

Dale A. Blyth   *issue*
Joyce A. Walker   *editors*

JOSSEY-BASS™
An Imprint of
WILEY

RETHINKING PROGRAMS FOR YOUTH IN THE MIDDLE YEARS
Dale A. Blyth, Joyce A. Walker (eds.)
New Directions for Youth Development, No. 112, Winter 2006
Gil G. Noam, Editor-in-Chief

Microfilm copies of issues and articles are available in 16mm and 35mm, as well as microfiche in 105mm, through University Microfilms Inc., 300 North Zeeb Road, Ann Arbor, Michigan 48106-1346.

NEW DIRECTIONS FOR YOUTH DEVELOPMENT (ISSN 1533-8916, electronic ISSN 1537-5781) is part of The Jossey-Bass Psychology Series and is published quarterly by Wiley Subscription Services, Inc., A Wiley Company, at Jossey-Bass, 989 Market Street, San Francisco, California 94103-1741. POSTMASTER: Send address changes to New Directions for Youth Development, Jossey-Bass, 989 Market Street, San Francisco, California 94103-1741.

SUBSCRIPTIONS cost $80.00 for individuals and $195.00 for institutions, agencies, and libraries. Prices subject to change. Refer to the order form at the back of this issue.

EDITORIAL CORRESPONDENCE should be sent to the Editor-in-Chief, Dr. Gil G. Noam, McLean Hospital, 115 Mill Street, Belmont, MA 02478.

Cover photograph by Meg Takamura/Getty Images

www.josseybass.com

BICENTENNIAL
1807
⊛WILEY
2007
BICENTENNIAL

THE WILEY BICENTENNIAL—KNOWLEDGE FOR GENERATIONS

*E*ach generation has its unique needs and aspirations. When Charles Wiley first opened his small printing shop in lower Manhattan in 1807, it was a generation of boundless potential searching for an identity. And we were there, helping to define a new American literary tradition. Over half a century later, in the midst of the Second Industrial Revolution, it was a generation focused on building the future. Once again, we were there, supplying the critical scientific, technical, and engineering knowledge that helped frame the world. Throughout the 20th Century, and into the new millennium, nations began to reach out beyond their own borders and a new international community was born. Wiley was there, expanding its operations around the world to enable a global exchange of ideas, opinions, and know-how.

For 200 years, Wiley has been an integral part of each generation's journey, enabling the flow of information and understanding necessary to meet their needs and fulfill their aspirations. Today, bold new technologies are changing the way we live and learn. Wiley will be there, providing you the must-have knowledge you need to imagine new worlds, new possibilities, and new opportunities.

Generations come and go, but you can always count on Wiley to provide you the knowledge you need, when and where you need it!

WILLIAM J. PESCE
PRESIDENT AND CHIEF EXECUTIVE OFFICER

PETER BOOTH WILEY
CHAIRMAN OF THE BOARD

Contents

Editors' Notes

AT THE HEART OF THIS SPECIAL ISSUE lie our questions about how to rethink out-of-school learning opportunities in ways that better meet the developmental needs of early adolescents and utilize what we know about quality programs. Although the field has and is actively examining the issue of what after-school programs and other learning opportunities in the nonschool hours should look like for youth aged nine to fifteen years,[1] we chose to orient this issue on the topic around some of the learning from our recent experiences creating and leading a statewide effort to support community-based and school-linked nonformal learning opportunities for youth in all our communities. As coeditors working at a university-based statewide youth development intermediary whose overarching goal is to make a measurable difference in the quality, availability, and impact of such learning opportunities, our goal for this issue was to draw together our insights from our statewide work, current research, and practitioner experience in a way that makes sense for our everyday work and also pushes our thinking about what is necessary and possible as we move into the future.

In 2003, with encouragement from a range of partners and funders, the University of Minnesota president appointed the Minnesota Commission on Out-of-School Time that we, along with Ann Lochner, had the opportunity to staff. The charge to the commission was to "create a vision and strategies to ensure every Minnesota youth access to opportunities for learning and development during the nonschool hours."[2] This work and the various studies and discussions it spawned have shaped our thinking and approach to out-of-school time and after-school opportunities for youth.

NEW DIRECTIONS FOR YOUTH DEVELOPMENT, NO. 112, WINTER 2006 © WILEY PERIODICALS, INC.
Published online in Wiley InterScience (www.interscience.wiley.com) • DOI: 10.1002/yd.188

Consequently, the frameworks, perspectives, theories, and examples used in this volume reflect our efforts to both understand and guide such work.

At the heart of that work is the variety of activities for youth during the second decade of life that are commonly referred to as programs. Although the issue of naturally occurring learning opportunities in communities kept coming up, most of the attention focused on how to better understand the role of intentional structured youth programs; how they operate; what they need to efficiently and effectively offer high-quality, easily accessed, positive-impact opportunities for and with youth; and how to build public support and stable and sustainable funding for them. Based on this experience, and not wishing to tell just one state's story, we selected authors and articles that focused on programs for youth in the middle of the first two decades who are transitioning out of care and beginning more extensive journeys into their communities.

The nearly two years of commission work deepened our understanding of the hopes and concerns of citizens, policymakers, agency directors, government representatives, parents, and young people. It raised some old ideas and some new challenges. On one hand, we confronted some community assumptions about youth programs that surprised us. Relative to what Quinn has called a long-standing but newly self-conscious field of youth development,[3] much of the public assumes nothing much has changed from the previous century when programs were framed around content and organized by largely private, mission-driven organizations. People seem to believe things are going just fine. Others expressed the belief that the discretionary time of youth in the middle years is almost solely the responsibility of parents. Others see after-school programs as enrichment, a nonessential option for those who choose to take part and are willing to pay for it. Still others affirm the care and structure early childhood programs provide but stop short of equally appropriate support for older youth.

We had some of our own assumptions with which to deal. We in the field take for granted things that many parents, community leaders, and the general public do not. We learned that we need to better bolster arguments for active support for young people over their first two decades. Many had never considered that models of care for young children increasingly do not fit for the youth in the middle years who expect voice and choice as the price of participation. The idea that "if you build it, they will come" is losing ground with young adolescents, who appropriately want to help build it and have a voice in running it as well. We assumed some public understanding of after-school programs as intentional learning environments that effectively use different structures of teaching and learning, different pedagogies and curriculum, and different adult-youth relationships to achieve their goals. These initial misreadings of public sentiment led to our interest in reframing out-of-school-time issues and developing the diet-and-exercise analogy to clarify the meaning of youth development.

This commission experience reinforced, above all else, the complexity of improving the quality, access, and impact of programs while simultaneously trying to influence the formation of policy, systems, and funding streams to support this youth development work. Clearly the work is not solely about programs. Nonetheless, we found that understanding what goes on in community-based and school-linked programs at the point of service where young people engage with learning opportunities is central to most discussions of systems, policy, and funding efforts.

This special issue has three sections. The first focuses on framing youth development programs for the public and the field. Lochner and Bales describe the research strategy and action items that were undertaken to reframe the out-of-school-time issue in order to build public support among citizens and voters. Blyth urges the youth development field to consider a new paradigm to help the public and the youth development colleagues understand the essential elements of development and learning fostered by structured nonformal learning experiences in the nonschool hours.

The second addresses the learning opportunities in the nonschool hours from the perspective of youth and their parents. Here issues of choice and opportunities for all are raised alongside observations of the capacity of resource-rich and resource-depleted communities and neighborhoods. Marczak, Dworkin, Skuza, and Beyer report on the preferences of youth and parents as they select out-of-school-time activities to enrich their free time. Saito steps back a bit further, seeking information about program activities from nonparticipants. She also makes observations about the ability of communities to support a substantial variety of choices for young people. In her typology of community resources, she echoes the commission's observation that the scope and scale of these programs depend on the ability of communities to provide resources to support programs for the discretionary time of young people.

Third, the theory and research chapters focus on program intentionality, program outcomes, program quality, and professional leadership. Walker explores a program development model that emphasizes intentionality, engagement, and goodness of fit for success. Smith, Akiva, Arrieux, and Jones describe the High/Scope model of assessing quality at the point of service. Their model is offered as a method of evaluating a program or of self-assessment for continuous quality improvement. Last, Walker and Larson identify from their research a range of practice dilemmas that test the mettle of youth development program staff in their daily dealings with young people. The question of how to prepare program staff to generate choices and decide on courses of action are not answered, but the challenge of dealing with complex, layered dilemmas in everyday work with youth rings true to any practitioner.

What does all of this rethinking add up to? A heightened awareness of the essential importance of learning and development in the nonschool hours and the need for a community commitment to support and fund these opportunities on behalf of youth today and community leadership in the future. One way or another, young people in their middle years seek involvement and are poised to take part in learning opportunities that engage their talents, build their skills, and offer a chance to do real work in the real world that makes a real difference.

Notes

1. For examples, see Quinn, J. (1999). Where need meets opportunity: Youth development programs for early teens. *Future of Children: When School Is Out, 9*(2), 96–116; Westmoreland, H., Little, P., & Gannett, E. (2006, Fall). Exploring quality in afterschool programs for middle school-age youth. *Afterschool Review, 1*(1), 8–13.

2. Minnesota Commission on Out-of-School Time. (2005, May). *Final report: Journeys into community: Transforming youth opportunities for learning and development.* At http://www.MNCOST.org

3. Quinn. (1999).

4. Minnesota Commission on Out-of-School Time. (2005, May). Charge to the commission.

Dale A. Blyth
Joyce A. Walker
Editors

DALE A. BLYTH *is the associate dean for youth development at the University of Minnesota, where he directs the Center for 4-H and Community Youth Development and provides statewide leadership for the youth development program area of the University of Minnesota Extension Service.*

JOYCE A. WALKER *is a professor and community youth development educator at the Center for 4-H and Community Youth Development at the University of Minnesota, where she also gives leadership to the Youth Development Leadership M.Ed. Program in the College of Education and Human Development.*

NEW DIRECTIONS FOR YOUTH DEVELOPMENT • DOI: 10.1002/yd

Executive Summary

Chapter One: Framing youth issues for public support

Ann Lochner, Susan Nall Bales

The insights from one state illustrate the challenges of working to shape public will to favor support for out-of-school learning opportunities for youth ages nine to fifteen. With the leadership of the Frameworks Institute, local and national research and reframing concepts were used to develop a strategy to help advocates communicate the value of these learning opportunities in ways the public is less likely to dismiss out of hand. Messages reinforcing the developmental need to practice skills using the illustration of brain architecture and emphasizing the important role of community contribution on future leadership proved to be important aspects of the communication strategy.

Chapter Two: Toward a new paradigm for youth development

Dale A. Blyth

Although practitioners and researchers continue to shape the emerging field of youth development, we have still not found a clear and compelling way to talk about our work to family members, the public, and policymakers. The diet-and-exercise analogy presented here compares features essential for good health with comparable features affecting positive youth development. The

NEW DIRECTIONS FOR YOUTH DEVELOPMENT, NO. 112, WINTER 2006 © WILEY PERIODICALS, INC.
Published online in Wiley InterScience (www.interscience.wiley.com) • DOI: 10.1002/yd.189

7

effects of the inputs or nutrients of a healthy diet are magnified when the individual makes a commitment to exercise. Likewise, the impact of teaching and developmental supports is magnified when young people become actively engaged in their own learning and development.

Chapter Three: What's up? What young teens and parents want from youth programs

Mary S. Marczak, Jodi Dworkin, Jennifer Skuza, Janet Beyer

Young teens and their parents clearly state that the "if you build it, they will come" approach, even if it is well built, is only part of the solution for engaging young people in learning opportunities. Interviews with youth and parents explore what they are doing and what they say they want in their nonschool hours. Opportunities that are flexible, less structured, and more leisure-based emerge as priorities. Although relatively content with the options currently available to them, when pressed, youth and families want more connections between people and age groups as well as more of the free-spirited, organic activities likely to emerge in neighborhoods and communities.

Chapter Four: Beyond access and supply: Youth-led strategies to captivate young people's interest in and demand for youth programs and opportunities

Rebecca N. Saito

Increasing access, even increasing supply, may not be sufficient to attract young teens who do not typically participate in youth programs. Several youth mapping projects in rural and urban communities have led to these conclusions: youth do not know what is available even in their own neighborhoods, young teens have a strong voice in how they spend their discretionary time, and we need to learn how to market youth programs much more effectively. This author reviews important findings from youth community-mapping experiences and showcases a project attempting to move beyond access and supply issues to increasing young people's interest and engagement in community youth development programs.

Chapter Five: Intentional youth programs: Taking theory to practice

Joyce A. Walker

Early adolescents benefit most from program opportunities where they can be actively engaged in their own learning and development and where there is a good fit between their developmental needs and the intentional learning opportunities provided by the program. The theoretical framework presented here suggests that the two most important features of an engaging youth program are an intentional ethos of youth development and an intentional strategy to design and implement developmentally appropriate learning experiences. Practical examples from research and community practice are used to illustrate program strategies for early adolescents that emphasize intentional thought, decisions, and actions every step of the way.

Chapter Six: Improving quality at the point of service

Charles Smith, Tom Akiva, Dominique Arrieux, Monica M. Jones

The authors provide a research-based construct of youth program quality that differentiates safety, support, interaction, and engagement, four important issues for practitioners working with youth in the middle years. They describe two tools that have helped direct staff to be intentional about creating offerings that are appropriate for early adolescents: the focusing idea of point-of-service quality and the technology of observational assessment. They describe how these tools can be used to create cultures of accountability and intentionality that extend across program levels.

_____

Chapter Seven: Dilemmas of youth work: Balancing the professional and personal

Kathrin C. Walker, Reed W. Larson

Being an effective and intentional youth practitioner involves more than planning. It includes being able to react intelligently to the many difficult situations that arise. Practitioners in out-of-school and after-school settings regularly confront complex dilemmas that emerge in their daily work. They face situations where competing objectives, values, and warrants come into conflict, situations that can pit the developmental needs of youth, ethical concerns, administrative requirements, and other considerations against each other. Using examples from their research that weigh professional and personal judgments, the authors illustrate the complexity of these practice dilemmas and the considerations program staff included as they responded to these challenging situations.

Communicating effectively about the community's role in promoting positive youth development is critical to generating public support for quality youth programs.

1

Framing youth issues for public support

Ann Lochner, Susan Nall Bales

RESEARCH HAS CONFIRMED SHORT- and long-term positive effects of quality youth development programs. Young people who participate in structured developmental programs have better school attendance, better grades, more positive attitudes toward school, and higher aspirations for postsecondary education.[1] Adults who as young people participate in activities outside of the regular school day are more likely to trust their parents, settle in stable relationships, be employed, report being happy with their lives, and be active in their communities.[2] Despite this evidence, policies supporting these programs are inadequate due in part to limited public understanding about the developmental process and the role of quality youth development programs during the middle years. This conclusion prompted the Minnesota Commission on Out-of-School Time and its Minnesota collaborators to sponsor a Frame-Works Institute study of the attitudes of Minnesota citizens and parents toward youth and youth programs and how to effectively increase their understanding about and support for positive youth development programs.

NEW DIRECTIONS FOR YOUTH DEVELOPMENT, NO. 112, WINTER 2006 © WILEY PERIODICALS, INC.
Published online in Wiley InterScience (www.interscience.wiley.com) • DOI: 10.1002/yd.190

This article highlights how a youth policy commission came to identify the need for public will building as a priority in promoting positive youth policies. We review recommendations that emerged from a research study exploring how the policy conversation about youth and youth programs could be successfully reframed. We also identify common dominant frames that negatively influence the way people think about youth issues and alternate frames that evoke a different way of thinking that is more supportive of positive policy solutions. Implications of reframes for effectively communicating about youth and intentional programs so vital to their optimal development are demonstrated.

Minnesota Commission on Out-of-School Time

The Minnesota Commission on Out-of-School Time was convened in December 2004 by University of Minnesota President Robert Bruininks as part of his Presidential Initiative on Children, Youth, and Families. Commissioners were experts in the fields of child and adolescent development as well as representatives of business; philanthropy; youth development programs; county, state, and tribal governments; and youth. The commission's charge was to create a vision and strategies to ensure every Minnesota youth access to opportunities supportive of his or her optimal development during nonschool hours. The commission's work was reinforced by research confirming the critical role of high-quality out-of-school opportunities in assuring that young people reach adulthood ready to assume roles as responsible community members and leaders. Through a series of work groups, meetings, dialogues, and a youth caucus, this intergenerational group identified a vision for out-of-school time in Minnesota that includes key issues facing families, young people, program providers, and policymakers as well as a series of recommendations.[3]

Throughout commission deliberations, communities were viewed as the critical intersection where key developmental influences converge during the middle years. Building on the foundation established by families during early childhood and extending beyond the purview of academic learning, communities increasingly become the nexus of opportunities through which young people chart their course through childhood and adolescence. It was acknowledged that considerable public support would be required for communities to provide an adequate supply of quality programs replete with relationships and experiences integral to the middle years of development.

Commissioners recognized that despite the enormously high stakes for the development of young people and the vitality of their communities, access, availability, and quality of out-of-school opportunities across Minnesota communities varied dramatically. Commissioners began to see connections between uneven quality among programs, program funding cuts, insufficient legislative attention, and a general shortage of good information about youth development and the importance of developmentally supportive programs. Increasingly, attention focused on the need to engage the public and policymakers in seeing the merit of positive developmental opportunities for all young people. Commissioners called for a public will-building effort to engage the public at large and voting citizens in Minnesota communities in understanding the added value of intentional community-based learning and development opportunities for young people.

Given the limited research on public attitudes about out-of-school and after-school programs, learning more about how Minnesotans think about the role of these programs in the development of young people was deemed a critical first step in reaching out to the public. The FrameWorks Institute was engaged to design a research study that would clarify dominant frames influencing public attitudes regarding youth, their development, their developmental needs, and the policies and programs that would have an impact on their success.[4]

FrameWorks Institute

The FrameWorks Institute works with nonprofit and philanthropic organizations interested in stimulating a broader conversation about the causes and solutions associated with a variety of social issues. The past decade of research in the social and cognitive sciences strongly suggests that the challenge of communicating about social issues requires an understanding of the conceptual frames that ordinary people bring to any given policy discussion.

Using a multimethod, multidisciplinary approach to communications research, called Strategic Frame Analysis, FrameWorks documents dominant frames in public discourse, determines their impact on public opinion and policy preferences, and suggests how public thinking can be redirected (reframed) to support positive policy solutions more in keeping with the recommendations of scholarly research and policy experts.

Frames

From the perspective of Strategic Frame Analysis, public understanding of an issue depends on its association with what Walter Lippmann called "the pictures in our heads." Put simply, people use mental shortcuts to make sense of the world. These mental shortcuts rely on "frames": a small set of internalized concepts and values that allow us to accord meaning to unfolding events and new information. Put another way, frames are "*organizing principles* that are socially *shared* and *persistent* over time, that work *symbolically* to meaningfully *structure* the social world" (italics in the original).[5] These frames can be triggered by various elements, such as language choices and different messengers or images. Each of these communications elements, therefore, may have a profound influence on decision outcomes.[6] The result is that policy preferences and attributions of responsibility vary dramatically depending on the way an issue is framed or defined for the public. Framing gun control as an issue of individual autonomy, for example, leads to very different conclusions from those evoked when the same issue is framed as a matter of public health. And the same individuals, exposed to these different frames, can alternate between opposing views.

When it comes to public affairs, people get most information from the news media, which over time sets up a framework of expectation about issues, or dominant frames. Habits of thought are developed that configure incoming information to conform to established frames, becoming mental shortcuts for processing new information. Understanding is thus frame-based rather than fact-based. Even when confronted with new facts about an issue, most people will rely on the frame most familiar to them rather than contest that frame by accepting the new facts as truth. This is important in a number of respects: first, it tends to preclude new understanding of an issue, but more subtly, these frames also establish who is responsible for fixing any given social problem.

The social science literature of the past two decades has confirmed that the perspective from which stories are told, or how they are framed, is a powerful influence in assigning responsibility for an issue or problem. Understanding which frames advance which policy options (solutions) is critical to effective communications.

Political psychologist Shanto Iyengar describes two types of frames that are frequently used in the news media. Episodic frames (which dominate U.S. television newscasts) depict public issues through the lens of concrete occurrences that happen in a specific time and place, such as crime reports. In most cases, the story is narrowly focused on the individuals involved—the victim or the perpetrator—and resembles a case study. The individual is assigned responsibility. By contrast, thematic frames place public issues in a broader context, identifying the circumstances in the community or systems that contributed to the problem. Using the crime report example, a thematic frame would describe the conditions in the community or shortcomings of current policies as well as related trends, a distinctly different story from the episodic focus on life stories or salient characteristics of perpetrator and victim. Experimental research demonstrates that thematic frames more effectively engage the public in policy solutions.[7]

Thus, Strategic Frame Analysis focuses on broad societal conditions and systems responsible for social issues, recognizing that social issues require admission of a problem to the public arena for it to be prioritized for policy solutions—a long-term process. This approach distinguishes Strategic Frame Analysis from more typical marketing, public service advertising, persuasion, and public relations campaigns that target individual behavior and use cryptic messages in communication with consumers over a shorter time span, with the goal of stimulating individual actions or behaviors. And in seeking to align expert and lay understanding of an issue, Strategic Frame Analysis takes on the complex job of translating the thematic understanding of social issues into simpler terms without losing the important frame elements of context and attribution of responsibility.

Focus of Minnesota research

The Minnesota research built on a broader research base established through a more extensive national study of public attitudes about adolescent development conducted for the W. T. Grant Foundation from 1999 to 2001.[8] FrameWorks tested those earlier findings with the Minnesota public and posed additional questions to probe possible approaches for reframing the role of community in advancing youth development in the state. Among the earlier findings (for W. T. Grant cited above) was one that proved of special interest in Minnesota: the predominantly negative perception of youth held by many Americans. The conclusions from this earlier study portray mixed attitudes about young people influenced in large part by the media. Today, youth are viewed as being fundamentally different from youth in the past, and the difference is attributed by adults to declining values. Parents are seen as the culprits for this negative trend and are held primarily, if not exclusively, responsible for the well-being of their own children and youth. Good parenting is defined narrowly as protection from physical harm and the negative influences of peers and community. Perhaps most notable is the belief that youth are fully formed rather than progressing through a predictable stage in human development during which behavior and decision making are profoundly affected by documented changes in brain architecture.

Methods for understanding and testing public frames about youth

The first step in any effort to engage the public in a political or social issue requires a descriptive analysis of the information people have available to them. Given most people's relative unfamiliarity with most social and political issues, this requires an understanding of the way an issue has been portrayed in the news, our culture's primary political storyteller. Secondarily, analysts attempt to discern, using qualitative research methods, the degree to which these news frames have been internalized by citizens and the extent that they can remember and reason based on the stories taught to them by the media. In the case of youth development, where some familiarity with the issue is presumed, communications scholars attempt to identify missing pieces of information that prevent ordinary people from learning new ways to think about an issue. This is especially pertinent for issues about which the public is asked to understand complicated scientific phenomena and to reach policy judgments based on that understanding—whether this relates to global warming, ozone depletion, or human development.

Building on FrameWorks's earlier work on youth development, as well as extensive work on early child development,[9] a series of hypotheses or testable propositions was developed to guide the work in Minnesota. These included the following:

- The dominance of parental responsibility is likely to undermine initial support for public investments in youth programs.
- The absence of an identifiable social good to which after-school programs are a means will reinforce the identity of the issue as private for most people.
- Positive community actors and influences will require conscientious reinforcement if they are to establish community as a locus for positive effects on the lives of youth.
- Framing after-school programs narrowly as crime prevention is unlikely to result in greater support for quality developmental programs.

NEW DIRECTIONS FOR YOUTH DEVELOPMENT • DOI: 10.1002/yd

- The absence of a concrete metaphor—or simplifying model[10]—will prove a stumbling block in teaching the public new information.

To test these propositions, and to determine whether they could be overcome using speculative reframes, FrameWorks's Minnesota research was structured as a two-tiered information-gathering approach involving focus groups and cognitive elicitations in local communities.

Focus groups

Eight geographically representative focus groups were conducted in Minnesota, in addition to two groups dedicated exclusively to minority representation. Focus group members were chosen randomly to include "engaged citizens," or individuals who are likely to be voters and community contributors. A series of hypothetical news articles modeled after actual news reports was used as the stimulus for a series of discussions about youth and youth programs. Focus groups were designed to explore the following:

- How Minnesotans think in general about youth, their developmental needs, and types of policies and programs that affect them.
- What frames are most frequently used by adults when thinking about youth and the impact of these dominant frames on adults' consideration of policy proposals such as using public funds to expand after-school programs.
- Which alternative frames would prove effective in evoking a different way of thinking, one that is more supportive of positive policy solutions.

Cognitive elicitations

To validate and extend the focus group findings, one-on-one unstructured interviews were also conducted with twenty average Minnesota citizens and analyzed by a team of linguists and anthropologists associated with the FrameWorks Institute. These research subjects were recruited through an ethnographic networking process.

Findings on public attitudes

Minnesota research findings confirm the earlier youth development research conducted for W. T. Grant. As hypothesized, the public's dominant frame was one of personal and parental responsibility for youth that prevented people from according a public role for positive youth development in the form of after-school programs. When frames emphasizing the importance of protecting youth from crime were tested, adults were indeed willing to support after-school programs but not the quality developmental programs that research has demonstrated and social policy experts believe make a difference. Although there was limited awareness about the influence of community actors as influences on young people, Minnesotans remembered and reaffirmed the role of mentors when reminded of these actors in ways that did not displace the role of parents.

The Minnesota research also revealed three critical frame elements that can greatly aid in public reappraisals of youth programs: brain development in youth, the role of youth in community development, and the role of community in youth development. First, it is important to explain youth in developmental terms with an emphasis on the active phase of brain development activated by particular features of programs in which they are engaged. Second, people need to understand the critical link between positive youth development and the community, state, and nation's future viability. Minnesotans are likely to rethink their reaction to youth programs if these are understood in the context of community development. It is important to emphasize that high-quality youth programs provide the pathway through which communities are transformed, as are actively engaged young people. Investment in youth is investment in the vitality of communities. This kind of statement is likely to help Minnesotans see the end goal to which youth development is a necessary means. Third, it is in community settings that developmental opportunities take place. The use of strong, concrete developmental metaphors, like the stages of brain architecture that accompany development, helps people understand that young people are experiencing a predictable biological stage of growth and change that is interconnected with the environment of developmental opportunities available in their communities. This is dramatically different from their perceived identity, as documented in the previous FrameWorks's research: youth as "the other." In sum, a substantially different conversation can be had with Minnesotans about the importance of youth development if this topic is framed in terms of community and development, not risks, crime, and parental responsibility.

Youth messages reframed

As was illustrated in FrameWorks's research findings, engaging public support for positive youth development programs requires understanding of the developmental process, the role of intentional opportunities as essential developmental tools, and the role of communities as both the locus of intentional experiences and the ultimate destination for the developmental journey. FrameWorks's framing advice is instructive in guiding the creation of a more compelling story to engage the public in supporting positive policy solutions for young people:

- The solution is placed up front to indicate what readers should understand as the central need, reasons they should be concerned, and the change needed.
- The relationship between the role of parents, youth programs, and communities is made explicit by framing them as interconnected and interdependent.
- The developmental benefits of youth programs and how they support young people's developmental needs is made explicit by employing brain architecture as a simplifying model. This analogy describes the developmental construction work in which youngsters are engaged and portrays development during the middle years into adulthood as a biological phase through which all young people must navigate.

- Community is positioned as the place young people naturally navigate as their maturation process progresses and is the locus of developmental activities.
- The value of developmental opportunities is elevated when correlated with practicing roles they will later play as adults as integrated community members and contributors.

The Minnesota message is reframed as follows: The importance of providing essential experiences during out-of-school hours cannot be overstated in light of recent brain research about the critical role they play in the development of young people:

- Through experience, practice, and experimentation with roles they will later play as adults—such as teamwork, decision making, leadership, and community contribution—young people ensure the developmental connections needed to establish that these competencies are completed.
- This real-life skill building happens in communities in structured programs like 4-H or CampFire or activities in the wider community where parents and other adults serve as community guides for the developmental journey of young people.
- As children and youth engage in high-quality developmental experiences over time, they practice the skills they will need to become responsible adults and enhance the vitality of their communities in the process: a win-win situation.

Lessons learned: Perspectives about framing youth issues

Advocates for intentional youth programs and those who document their benefits have long wondered about the shallowness of public support. Whereas people say they would support youth programs, that consensus dissolves in the face of argument for reasons that the FrameWorks's research reveals.

As illustrated in FrameWorks's research findings, generating wide public support for positive youth development programs requires grounding the issue in an understanding of the developmental process of adolescence, explaining the role of intentional opportunities as essential tools for growth and development, and positioning communities as both the locus of intentional experiences and the ultimate destination for the developmental journey.

Clearly, this research argues, positive youth programs must be framed in terms of the larger societal benefits that accrue from youth engagement in these programs. In addition, by helping Minnesotans understand how development works and how youth programs of various quality support or impede adolescent development, policy advocates can engage in the important work of public education.

Notes

1. Huang, D., Gribbons, B., Kim, K. S., Lee, C., & Baker, E. L. (2000). *A decade of results: The impact of the LA's BEST afterschool enrichment initiative on subsequent student achievement and performance.* Los Angeles: University of California at Los Angeles Graduate School of Education and Information Studies, Center for the Study of Evaluation; Hamilton, L. S., & Klein, S. P. (1998). *Achievement test score gains among participants in the foundation's school-age enrichment program.* Santa Monica, CA: Rand Corporation.

2. Gambone, M. A., Klem, A. M., & Connell, J. P. (2002). *Finding out what matters for youth: Testing key links in a community action framework for youth development.* Philadelphia: Youth Development Strategies and the Institute for Research and Reform in Education; Connell, J. P., Gambone, M. A., & Smith, T. J. (2000). Youth development in community settings: Challenges to our field and our approach. In *Youth development issues, challenges, and directions* (pp. 281–299). Philadelphia: Public/Private Ventures.

3. Minnesota Commission on Out-of-School Time. (2005). *Journeys into community: Transforming youth opportunities for learning and development.* Minneapolis: University of Minnesota. http://www.mncost.org

4. Bales, S. N. (2005). *Making the case for youth programs: The Minnesota research.* A FrameWorks Message Memo. Washington, DC: FrameWorks Institute; Bales, S. N. (2005). *Minnesotans talk about youth issues.* Washington, DC: FrameWorks Institute.

5. Reese, S. D., Grandy, O. H., Jr., & Grant, A. E. (2001). *Framing public life: Perspectives on media and our understanding of the social world.* Mahwah, NJ: Erlbaum.

6. Iyengar, S. (1987). *News that matters: Television and American opinion.* Chicago: University of Chicago Press.

7. Iyengar, S. (1991). *Is anyone responsible? How television frames political issues.* Chicago: University of Chicago Press.

8. Bales, S. N. (2001). *Reframing youth issues for public consideration and support.* Washington, DC: FrameWorks Institute.

9. Bales, S. N. (2005). *Talking early child development and exploring the consequences of frame choices.* Washington, DC: FrameWorks Institute.

10. Aubrun, A, Grady, J., & Bales, S. N. *Topic: Opening up the black box: A case study in simplifying models.* Washington, DC: FrameWorks Institute.

ANN LOCHNER *provides leadership for the Applied Research Collaborative on Youth Development at the University of Minnesota Center for 4-H and Community Youth Development. She previously served as director of the Minnesota Commission on Out-of-School Time.*

SUSAN NALL BALES *is the president and founder of the nonprofit Frame-Works Institute. She is a contributing member of the National Scientific Council on the Developing Child at Harvard University.*

*A diet-and-exercise analogy is proposed to provide
a new way of understanding the complexity of youth
development and the increased role of youth in
shaping that development during the middle years.*

2

Toward a new paradigm for youth development

Dale A. Blyth

THE FIELD OF YOUTH DEVELOPMENT is based on a long tradition of youth work practice, a body of research on adolescent development, an increasing understanding of developmental processes, and work in related applied fields like education and child care. Whereas multiple lists have emerged describing what comprises or is needed for youth development,[1] the field lacks a dynamic and appropriately complex theory or paradigm that captures what is known and stimulates new insights. A paradigm shift that incorporates changes in basic assumptions and a new understanding of the dynamics involved is critical to examining how after-school and other nonformal learning programs can meet the needs of youth in the middle years (ages nine to fifteen). During these years, dynamic new biological, cognitive, social, and broader ecological forces in the community shape learning and development. Any new paradigm, especially one useful for applied work, must recognize these dynamic forces, the larger community ecology, and the critical role of youth themselves in creating, shaping, and interpreting the opportunities they experience.

NEW DIRECTIONS FOR YOUTH DEVELOPMENT, NO. 112, WINTER 2006 © WILEY PERIODICALS, INC.
Published online in Wiley InterScience (www.interscience.wiley.com) • DOI: 10.1002/yd.191

In this chapter, I articulate six fundamental tenets of youth development, propose an analogy to help elucidate the dynamic dimensions of the field, and then explore the implications of this analogy for creating a new paradigm. My thinking grows out of over thirty years in the field of adolescent and youth development as a researcher, author, educator, sociologist, and developmental psychologist as well as an administrator of a major youth program and a university-based center focused on bridging research and practice. The tenets are not my unique creation, but when combined and examined in light of a new analogy built around parallels to the elements of diet and exercise, they can provide insight into the importance of out-of-school-time opportunities for learning and development, especially during the middle years. In the process, I hope to reframe how researchers, practitioners, program designers, and policymakers think about youth's development and perhaps take a few steps toward developing a new, more dynamic, and adequately complex paradigm to guide future work.

Six tenets of youth development

The first tenet of youth development is that it happens whether planned or accidental. Youth have experiences in time and place that influence how they grow, learn, and develop. Their development is a complex accumulation of these everyday experiences. Furthermore, not all such experiences are occurring in the context of family or school, where most research to date has focused. Much of it occurs in a variety of nonformal and informal community and program contexts with (or without) adults and other youth.

Second, development is cumulative and becomes increasingly more positive or more negative depending on the nature of the experiences and how they are processed by the youth. It is not enough to simply provide a specific experience if one wishes to shape development. Rather, one needs to guide the menu from which youth select experiences, the ways they engage in those experiences, and to whom they turn to draw meaning from them.

NEW DIRECTIONS FOR YOUTH DEVELOPMENT • DOI: 10.1002/yd

Third, some proportion of these daily experiences are, or at least could be, influenced by and intentionally designed to have a positive effect on the young person's development. Currently too many experiences are simply left to chance, market forces (who can reach the youth with the products and services they wish to push), or economic and community factors. As illustrated by Karen Pittman's cube of time, place, and outcomes,[2] American society and families, although deliberate about very young children, are considerably less focused on these factors for school-age and adolescent youth beyond the school day. Although youth development clearly does not just happen in programs or structured experiences, it is possible to significantly influence development and learning by shaping a portion of youth's daily experiences in community more deliberately. Youth policy, program design, and the work of practitioners can and should do just that. And, as the chapter by Lochner and Bales in this issue suggests (Chapter One), this is what the public has to increasingly understand if public will is to support healthy youth development.[3]

Fourth, the contexts in which these everyday experiences occur change significantly as youth age. This is especially the case when youth reach the middle years (ages nine to fifteen) when changes in school settings, family relationships, peers, and a broader set of community contexts often influence the nature of these experiences and who else is present. Young people move from environments that emphasize care to those emphasizing challenge and participation. They spend more time in community contexts during the more than 1,800 hours of nonschool (and often nonfamily) time they have each year.

Fifth, as young people grow older, they have an increasingly larger voice in the choice of their discretionary experiences. Whereas families and school systems can and do continue to influence what youth experience, youth come to have a significant say in where they are, what they are doing, and with whom they are doing it. Youth in America have increasingly larger amounts of discretion at younger ages and, for a significant number of youth, a disturbing lack of both positive opportunities from which to choose and adequate support for making those choices. It is hard to influence the accumulation of everyday experiences unless one can influence those who choose them: the youth themselves, who increasingly vote with their feet by leaving or not becoming engaged.[4]

Sixth, the changes in physical, cognitive, and social development that occur during these years can fundamentally alter both the nature of an experience and how experiences are processed. For example, the new research on brain growth during adolescence, particularly the "blossoming and pruning" that appears to occur in the areas of the brain that deal with executive functions and impulse control, can have major implications for both what experiences youth choose and how they process those experiences.[5]

Although these six tenets are fairly well understood,[6] they do not provide a solid theory to help guide future research, application, or policy. What is missing is a more dynamic way of understanding them in relation to each other and to other aspects of development and community ecology. This is where a new analogy may prove useful, especially one with something that is both commonly understood and yet adequately complex.

A new analogy for youth development

A new way to frame youth development and learning using a diet-and-exercise analogy is described in this section. This analogy emerged over time as a result of attempts to clarify these complex phenomena for a variety of largely nonresearch and nontheoretical audiences of parents, funders, and practitioners. What would happen if the field of youth development thought of its work in terms of nutrition and exercise and the ways in which everyday experiences provide opportunities to absorb needed "developmental nutrients"? Admitting that diet alone is not enough, what "developmental muscles groups" need exercising? How might such an analogy help to focus thinking in terms of health but not in terms of programs as treatments or pills? In this section, I provide a basic answer to these questions with reference to youth during the middle years and their use of out-of-school time.

The diet-and-exercise analogy, illustrated in Table 2.1, is built around an initial effort to define the developmental nutrients that youth need from their experiences for healthy development and the type of developmental muscle groups youth need to exercise during the middle years. The analogy is far from simple. It raises the question of whether the dynamic interplay of forces, and especially the role of the individual that makes losing weight and maintaining health so difficult, can provide an effective way to think creatively about programs for middle school youth. It suggests a shift in the framework that policymakers, practitioners, and the public

Table 2.1. Essential elements of a developmental nutrition-and-exercise analogy

Nutrition and exercise elements	*Analogous developmental elements*
Basic nutrients: proteins, fats, carbohydrates, vitamins, minerals	Developmental nutrients: caring people, constructive places, challenging possibilities
Meals: ways in which nutrients are consumed	Experiences available: whether formal programs, informal opportunities, or other specific experiences
Daily diet: what is actually eaten or the cumulative intake of nutrients	Use of out-of-school time: the cumulative intake of developmental nutrients through the experiences in which youth actually participate during these hours
Muscle systems: systems that need to be pushed to become or remain strong, such as the cardiovascular and musculoskeletal systems	Developmental "muscles": skills or talents that need to be learned, used, and challenged to grow strong, such as decision-making skills, social skills, impulse control, contribution, caring
Exercise: the extent to which muscles are worked	Engagement: the extent to which youth are learning and using different "developmental muscles" during experiences in which they participate
Overweight or obesity: result of excess amounts of poor food choices, too little exercise, or both	Risk behaviors: the extent to which an abundance of negative people, places, and possibilities and a lack of engagement result in poor outcomes

use from one too often guided by deficits and overly narrow views of education to one that is grounded in the cumulative nature of learning and development, is conscious of community contexts, and emphasizes young people's roles in their own development.

Developmental nutrients

In normal nutrition terms, nutrients are the essential elements that the body needs to absorb to live, generate energy, and grow. They consist of five broad classes—proteins, fats, carbohydrates, vitamins, and minerals—each of which is essential for life and used differently. In youth development, these might be analogous to the building blocks for development such as caring people, constructive places, and challenging possibilities.[7]

Caring people. People are both a part of the experiences that cause development and an aid to the processing of experiences so they can be used to grow developmentally and enhance learning. They include the adults who are part of everyday experiences, their same-age peers, and older and younger youth. They are family members, neighbors, coaches, and even strangers. The word *caring* is added to indicate that not all people all the time are developmental nutrients that aid growth. For example, results of a study conducted at Cornell University in a healthy rural community and a distressed urban neighborhood indicate the importance of differentiating positive and negative people in the lives of young people. In the rural community, the more adults a young person cited as important in his or her life, the less likely the youth was to engage in risk behaviors. The exact opposite was found in the distressed urban neighborhood. Why? Because the adults in the urban area were differentially unemployed adults hanging around the neighborhood and engaging in risky behaviors—essentially negative role models. Thus, it is not just the quantity of relationships or the age of the people but their characteristics—especially caring—that matters for development.

Constructive places. The second type of developmental nutrient is the places young people experience. Youth do not develop in a vacuum, and the nature of the places where they spend time matters. Whereas the degree of safety, both physical and emotional, is possibly the most researched characteristic, *constructive* is used here as the critical modifier. Constructive places not only are safe but also have positive norms and high expectations for the youth. Such places encourage exploration and prevent risk taking from becoming life threatening. These places contain resources and tools that aid learning and development. They are not necessarily expensive or highly structured places, but they are in the end constructive and most often deliberate. In short, places provide the setting in which the other developmental nutrients are absorbed, and like caring people, they matter for development.

Challenging possibilities. The final basic nutrient group of development is the challenging nature of the possibilities youth experience. Every experience contains some type or variety of possibilities. Experiences that offer challenging possibilities tend to engage the young person and help push forward his or her development. Development in many areas occurs because of the challenges they contain. Just like nutrients that the body processes, the challenges have to be developmentally appropriate for the youth to succeed and for an optimal contribution to development. Challenges that overwhelm the youth can be unhealthy, just as the lack of challenges can starve development.

Developmental meals. Young people's experiences, just like meals, contain a mixture of nutrients—people, places, and possibilities—that feed development. These elements of developmental nutrition can be deliberately built into programs and communities or left to chance. But knowing the meals available is not sufficient. One has to look at what food is consumed in a person's actual diet. Likewise, in the case of development, the daily diet of things in which youth are participating have a bigger influence than what is available. Just as some people rely on high-sugar or fast-food diets that are unhealthy (even when healthy alternatives are present), some youth experience people, places, and possibilities that are less healthy for their development.

What is the developmental diet of America's young people like? Are the high rates of risky behaviors, like the high rate of obesity in children, a sign of excesses in some developmental nutrients and deficiencies in others? Are we making it easy for youth to get too much of the wrong things and not enough of the developmentally useful experiences? In particular, for youth during the middle years, is society and public policy supporting families, communities, and young people themselves in creating a healthy developmental diet of caring people, constructive places, and challenging possibilities in ways that young people will choose to use? Such supports, by parents, schools, and communities, are especially important during the nonschool hours when discretionary choice is highest. More will be said about the implications of a developmental diet in the final section of this chapter, but first, just as in maintaining health, one must consider the other half of the analogy: exercise.

Strengthening developmental muscles

Whereas diet provides the nutrients the body needs to produce energy and build tissue, it is through muscles that the body is able to sustain itself and do things. Thus, although a developmental diet is important, it is only half the picture. The habits one differentially exercises affect the skills and attitudes that grow stronger. If young people do not build certain skills and use them regularly, those skills are less likely to develop further and may not be available when needed.

Unlike the three developmental nutrients, which seem straightforward and empirically based, defining developmental muscle groups is more difficult. What is suggested here has evolved as I have spoken to different groups and facilitated their use of the analogy to better understand and shape their programs and policies. Although there are undoubtedly many different ways to define developmental muscle groups (and only research using this analogy can help refine its utility), four are put forth here for illustration: thinking (including decision making and impulse control), mastery, connection, and contribution. Each is seen as an important outcome of development and something in which young people need to engage to strengthen these outcomes.

Thinking muscle group. Given the new brain research and the apparent value of a brain architecture model for public understanding (see Chapter One), the thinking muscles seem particularly important to middle age youth. The thinking "muscles" refer to the strength and functionality of the cognitive systems and to neural pathways that are well wired and efficient. Using

NEW DIRECTIONS FOR YOUTH DEVELOPMENT • DOI: 10.1002/yd

the blossoming-and-pruning analogy in brain development, exercising the thinking muscles helps to establish firm connections and efficient pathways while also trimming away old ways of thinking or acting that short-circuit good decision making. The particular muscles involved are things like decision making, problem solving, creativity, impulse control, ability to explore alternatives, take perspectives, and so forth. When one exercises these thinking muscles, one is practicing acting more rationally and learning to listen and manage emotions and input from the environment. Strong thinking muscles lead to healthy choices, temperate risk taking, and enhanced capacity to learn, understand, and use information.

Mastery muscle group. The mastery muscles are involved in helping strengthen a young person's competence and confidence. These help young people develop a sense of agency and mastery that strengthens their willingness to explore and learn more. One could argue that these are the muscles most affected by experiential learning. These muscles are exercised when young people engage in an area long enough to accomplish something valued. The National Academy of Sciences' report on community programs talks about the ways in which programs can and need to build a sense of mastery.[8] The importance of these muscles can be seen in the faces of young people who are proud of their accomplishments (whether from earning a 4-H ribbon or a scout merit badge), eager to learn more, and confident in the ways they present themselves.

Connection muscle group. The connection muscles are all about the nature and strength of connections with others and relate strongly to social development. It is not enough for youth to be surrounded by caring people (part of their developmental diet) if they themselves do not have the ability to make, use, and strengthen connections. Learning to accurately assess other people's perspectives and intentions, make new friends, and utilize one's social network to cope effectively with stress might all be indicators of strength in this muscle group. Helping young people develop skills in this area, skills too often ignored in schools, is critical and an area where after-school programs can excel.

Contribution muscle group. The contribution muscle group is about not only connecting to one or more communities or cultures but also contributing to making a difference. The muscles in this group could include building and using a set of values and engaging in ways that contribute to a greater good—through community service or service-learning projects and experiencing (through reflection) the joy that follows. The main point here is that young people who engage in such activities strengthen their skills in this area. These might also be called the citizenship muscles.

Healthy engagement. Just as the developmental nutrients are available to young people only when they participate in experiences where such developmental nutrients are present, the various muscle groups are exercised only when young people are actively engaged in appropriate experiences. Thus, according to this analogy, the choices young people make about what experiences they have (which developmental meals they eat) and how engaged they become in those experiences (their exercise routine) dramatically affect their overall developmental health. The value of this analogy for youth in the middle years is that it makes real the fact that they, like a dieter, are increasingly in control of what they participate in and how engaged they become. If opportunities during the out-of-school hours are to succeed, they must involve and engage youth. A youth's decision to participate differs from decisions by others to place a child in a care setting. In both cases, what youth do in the setting is important for learning and development, but in the case of youth in the middle years, it is particularly important because new muscle systems are developing rapidly. Just like early childhood education is essential for certain types of development, it appears as though the early adolescent years are periods of rapid brain growth and strengthening of various developmental muscles.

Implications of the move toward a new paradigm

The value of a new applied paradigm comes from its ability to shift the thinking of a variety of key stakeholders, create a more unified and integrated approach, and stimulate new insights into issues. In this section, the implications of the proposed analogy for public understanding, program development, daily practice, public policy, and research and evaluation (and those that practice each) are briefly noted. Often implications for one group also have implications for others as well.

Implications for public understanding

As suggested in the previous chapter in this issue, it is critical to find ways to help the public use frames that enhance understanding and that support appropriate action. The proposed analogy may help make explicit three things the public needs to better understand using an analogy they already know well. First, the analogy can help the public understand in simple terms what is needed for healthy development: the three basic developmental nutrients of caring people, constructive places, and challenging possibilities. The implication that enriching young people's lives with more of these essential elements is helpful is easily understood, as is the fact that a daily diet of uncaring people, destructive places, and no challenging possibilities for learning is not healthy. The model helps development become understood in terms similar to that of physical growth and health, thus engaging familiar investment frames.

A second implication is that participation in experiences matters. It is not sufficient to have a great developmental menu. One must actually take in the developmental nutrients, and that requires participation by the young person. Whether experiencing informal, naturally occurring opportunities rich in developmental nutrients or more formal programs designed to provide them, young people need to participate if they are to benefit. Sitting on the sidelines does not work. Even when the public sits out, the youth is taking in experiences. At a policy level, the implications of this may be to target programs in opportunity-depleted communities.

The third implication is that participation, or eating in terms of the analogy, is also not enough. Young people also need to exercise essential muscle groups if they are to develop strength in key areas.

Young people need to become engaged in their own learning and development and to develop habits that help them think more clearly, strengthen their sense of mastery, build strong connections, and contribute back to the community. Giving youth the opportunity, and the responsibility, for participating in things that are healthy as well as engaging in ways that contribute to their development is essential. It is especially essential as youth reach the middle years and beyond when an increasing proportion of the developmental nutrients they absorb and the habits they exercise are driven by their choices in an ever-expanding sense of community.

A fourth implication for the public is that what matters most is the combined accumulation of developmental nutrients—not a single program or meal—and the extent to which developmental muscles are exercised. This understanding counters the common desire for a magic pill or treatment program that will work miracles and emphasizes instead the importance of providing a range of opportunities in families, schools, and communities. These opportunities should be rich in developmental nutrients that youth can absorb and able to exercise key developmental muscles that strengthen their growth. This move way from a recipe or treatment approach that is overly simplistic to more of an awareness of the complexity of emerging beings is essential.

The public may begin to understand the complexity of development and the wide variety of developmental diet and exercise programs that one can use. Frames that oversimplify a complex reality often fail. At the same time, overly complex frames that help thinking but do not provide clear answers may contribute to a sense that nothing can be done. Only time will tell whether the type of diet-and-exercise frames proposed here or that evolve from this model can take advantage of the positive implications and avoid some of the downsides. What if public debates focused on the developmental diets desired for young people? What if communities could unite around a vision of what every youth needs and their responsibility for exercising key developmental muscles that matter? What if parents and communities began to realize that out-of-school-time opportunities are no longer the snack food of young people's developmental diet but an opportunity for a healthy and hearty developmental meal in the community that exercises needed skills?

Implications for practice

There are implications for program development and for practitioners as well.

Program development. When it comes to program development, there are three major implications. First, this approach may help program developers move away from a program-centered approach to a more youth-centered approach. Such a change would decrease the pressure to build a program with all the answers (and desired outcomes) and enhance a focus on how a program can contribute to the overall diet and exercise an individual experiences. Development does not happen just in programs, but programs can, when intentional, support youth's development in essential ways. This implication is perhaps best illustrated in Chapter Six in this issue in which Smith, Akiva, Arrieux, and Jones discuss the High/Scope Foundation work on program quality.

A second implication is the need to create developmentally appropriate programs, ones that have the right mix of developmental nutrients and opportunities to exercise key muscles. When programs are not developmentally appropriate, young people leave (or fail to become engaged). This suggests that program designs need to include elements that feed the next phase of growth. Just as the marketing world recognizes (and too often exploits) the fact that youth at age ten want to be like fifteen-year-olds, youth programs need to ensure developmental diets and exercise opportunities that encourage growth into the positive aspects of being older. When left to chance, this too often defaults to negative models of older behavior. Providing opportunities to take on increased responsibilities and make important choices in the safety of a constructive setting is invaluable to building up the thinking and connection muscles before they are needed in potentially problematic settings. This approach especially applies to offering challenging possibilities, arguably the developmental nutrient perhaps most missing in many American youth's lives today. In particular, youth in the middle years need programs and informal opportunities in community that challenge them to grow in positive ways and not just go along with others.

A third implication, and one with relevance to evaluation and policymakers as well, is that this analogy may help shift from an undue focus on long-range outcomes to a more appropriate emphasis on monitoring healthy processes and short-term outcomes. Whereas stopping drug use or closing the education gap (long-range outcomes) is important, no single program in school or during out-of-school time is going to fully accomplish it. Those that come closest are likely controlling a larger portion of the young person's daily diet and encouraging positive developmental exercise. Instead, monitoring programs to ensure that they are enriching the developmental nutrients young people take in and encouraging short-term exercise of key muscles are likely to be more effective in the long run. This is especially true once research has shown the effectiveness of such factors in reducing risks longer term. Monitoring the extent to which programs do the right thing, rather than focusing too heavily on inadequately funded summative evaluation of long-term outcomes, is an important shift needed in the field of youth development.

Practitioners. Practitioners are the paid professionals and volunteers who work directly with youth in a wide range of formal, nonformal, and informal settings. A major implication of this analogy is the importance of being intentional in key areas such as those outlined in the Walker chapter in this volume (Chapter Five). Practitioners who believe it is only about caring relationships may not provide sufficiently challenging opportunities to grow. An overly rich diet of caring relationships may also not encourage the exercise of important muscles. One might compare this with the faulty belief that teachers need to ensure that students have high self-esteem, whether earned or unearned. Helping practitioners understand the domains (developmental nutrients) and essential muscle groups that young people need to experience in age-appropriate ways can help them practice more intentionally and, one would predict, more effectively.[9]

The second implication for practitioners has to do with the value of structure. According to Allen Levine, professor and chair of the

University of Minnesota's Department of Food and Nutrition, it is often the structure that diet-and-exercise plans provide that make them effective.[10] Their structures help to narrow myriad choices and encourage ones that are likely healthier overall. Similarly, this analogy may help practitioners more appropriately structure their programs in ways that enhance their developmental nutrition and exercise key muscle groups—things that can enhance participation.

Finally, the complexity of this approach may encourage the growth of new ways to think about the professional preparation and development of practitioners. Checklists and licensing to ensure certain skills may be appropriate but insufficient if youth workers are operating in a more dynamic and ever-emerging reality, one that is constantly changed by the choices youth make and the increasing strength of their developmental muscles. What if practitioners were prepared to deal with practice dilemmas in ways that intentionally increased youth engagement and strengthened key muscles? What if practitioners were rewarded for the depth of youth engagement as well as their mere presence in the program? What if practitioners were better prepared to use structures that are flexible and developmentally appropriate for youth in the middle years?

Implications for policy

Although policy might do many things to encourage and support the implementation of the ideas above, there are four implications to highlight specifically for policymakers. First, this model could help policymakers move beyond a strictly care model (often common in early childhood) or formal education model (often dominating discussions of school-age and older youth) to a more developmental model. Each model has strengths and limitations as well as stakeholders that protect their turf. Public policy needs a frame that focuses on the development and learning of children and youth across the first two decades of life in a more holistic way that encourages a wide range of public, community, and personal investments. Efforts in early childhood are increasingly focusing on brain development and education rather than care alone as important. Widespread use of the developmental diet and exercise analogy and related empirical work may encourage a broader perspective for children as well as youth.

The second implication for policymakers is the simple introduction of exercising key muscles at developmentally appropriate times. Although advances in service-learning approaches and the value of problem solving and complex thinking can be found in certain public policies, few actually create systems or empower practitioners to challenge youth and enhance their muscles in critical areas of citizenship and critical-thinking skills.

A third implication for policy is the challenge to find ways to engage youth in meaningful roles and activities that exercise their developmental muscles and at the same time fundamentally change their role in community solutions. Although many can point to great examples of where youth have done this, few can point to policies that support it systematically. This could even by done in the area of out-of-school time itself. What if public policy not only created opportunities for youth to help out in after-school programs for younger children but also engaged youth in the mapping, creating, marketing, and reviewing of opportunities as a learning experience in itself?

A fourth implication for policy is the consequence of socially toxic environments, to use James Garbarino's language.[11] Because development and learning are cumulative and because they depend on developmental nutrients and the exercise of key developmental muscle groups, living in socially toxic or opportunity-depleted communities has consequences. Just as obesity is a problem of not only individual choices but also policies about advertising high-fat foods, youth development is about more than young people's choices or the creation of programs. It is also about ensuring healthy communities. And that requires policies at local, regional, state, and national levels that go beyond schools and youth program funding. What if public policy was required to examine the impact on youth, families, and communities the way businesses are required to assess environmental impact?

Implications for research and evaluation

Several of the implications noted above have parallel implications for those who study youth development and youth programs. A notable example is the need to research what happens in programs to encourage development and not just their long-term outcomes. The chapter by Walker and Larson (Chapter Seven) in this volume and others from that study are an excellent example. Moving to ways that help programs better monitor whether they have essential elements of quality, such as illustrated in the High/Scope article in this volume (Chapter Six), is another example.

Another implication of great relevance to researchers is the challenge of finding new metrics and new methods appropriate to a developmental diet-and-exercise paradigm. Is there a developmental analogue to the concept of calories or weight that are important to the diet-and-exercise approach to health? Could standards be set for the level of healthy developmental nutrients in different contexts, programs, or communities, just as foods now bear nutrition labels? Why should this occur? Why should it not occur? How might different metrics of new concepts introduced by the analogy help advance the field? Similarly, how do researchers and evaluators find better methods to describe, assess, and analyze the cumulative nature of developmental nutrients and exercise over time? Clearly, major changes in how researchers and evaluators think about empirically understanding youth development are needed, just as how others responsible for the areas noted above must also rethink their work. Whether that rethinking, as framed by the proposed diet-exercise analogy, is ultimately useful or distracting is not yet clear. That the field of youth development needs a new paradigm that better integrates what is known and informs application is clear.

Conclusion

In this chapter, I have focused on defining a new analogy for understanding youth development and drawing out its implications in many areas. The need for such a new model is particularly critical to understanding the development of middle age youth ages nine to fifteen—those who need more than care and more than formal education. Youth are increasingly thrust into making choices that affect their lives with less and less constructive practice or exercise in making them. Just as middle schools were an attempt to radically reform schools for this age group, youth development as a field needs a radically new approach, an approach that can be seen in some successful programs and communities but one that does not yet dominate how program designers, practitioners, policymakers, and researchers view this work. This analogy, with its promises and its blind spots, comes from years of trying to bridge what is known to create applications that are useful. Only time and use can determine if it is a shift toward a more dynamic paradigm. Until then, hopefully people will explore its possibilities for their own work and begin to reframe it for the future.

Notes

1. Benson, P. L. (1997). *All kids are our kids: What communities must do to raise caring and responsible children and adolescents.* San Francisco: Jossey-Bass; Benson, P. L., Leffert, N., Scales, P. C., & Blyth, D. A. (1998). Beyond the "village" rhetoric: Creating healthy communities for children and adolescents. *Applied Development Science, 2*(3), 138–159; Connell, J., Gambone, M. A., & Smith, T. (2000). Youth development in community settings. In G. Walker (Ed.), *Youth development: Issues, challenges and directions* (pp. 281–324). Philadelphia: Public/Private Ventures; Pittman, K., Ferber, T., & Irby, M. (2000). *Unfinished business: Further reflections on a decade of promoting youth development.* Takoma Park, MD: International Youth Foundation.

2. Pittman, K., Ferber, T., & Irby, M. (2000). *What fills the empty space? A tool for mapping youth investment.* Takoma Park, MD: International Youth Foundation.

3. Carnegie Council on Youth Development. (1992). *A matter of time: Risk and opportunity in the non-school hours.* Task Force on Youth Development and Community Programs and Carnegie Council on Adolescent Development. New York: Carnegie Corporation.

4. Westmoreland, H., Little, P.M.D., & Gannett, E. (2006, Fall). Exploring quality in afterschool programs for middle school-age youth. *Afterschool Review,* 8–13.

5. Walsh, D. (2004). *Why do they act that way? A survival guide to the adolescent brain for you and your teenager.* New York: Free Press.

6. Westmoreland et al. (2006).

7. Pittman, K. (1991). *Promoting youth development: Strengthening the role of youth-serving and community organizations.* Washington, DC: Center for Youth Development and Policy Research, Academy for Educational Development.

8. Eccles, J., & Gootman, J. A. (Eds.). (2002). *Community programs to promote youth development.* Washington, DC: National Academy Press.

9. Walker, J., Marczak, M., Blyth, D. A., & Borden, L. (2005). Designing intentional youth programs: Toward a theory of developmental intentionality. In J. Mahoney, R. Larson, & J. Eccles (Eds.), *Organized activities as contexts for development: Extracurricular activities, after-school and community programs.* Mahwah, NJ: Erlbaum.

10. From a personal conversation with Allen Levine in Fall 2005 discussing the value of a diet-and-exercise model for health and its possible utility as an analogy for development.

11. Garbarino, J. (1995). *Raising children in a socially toxic environment.* San Francisco: Jossey-Bass.

DALE A. BLYTH *is the associate dean for youth development at the University of Minnesota where he directs the Center for 4-H and Community Youth Development and provides statewide leadership for the youth development program area of the University of Minnesota Extension Service.*

Youth and parents provide critical voices regarding what young teens do, want, and need from out-of-school opportunities.

3

What's up? What young teens and parents want from youth programs

Mary S. Marczak, Jodi Dworkin,
Jennifer Skuza, Janet Beyer

"NO, NO, PUKE!" a ten-year-old girl stated emphatically when asked what she thought about participating in sports and other structured programs in her community. She went on to explain that she was a "girly girl" who just wanted to talk about girl things with her friends and maybe join gymnastics like her friends, if only her mother would not be afraid she would get hurt. Her response to our question about participation in structured activities was both unique and typical. Interviews with young teens offered many complex and often idiosyncratic reasons why they did or did not participate in structured activities (for example: personality, interest, attitudes about time use, personal and family life circumstances). However, there also exist common threads that should give one pause regarding the current wisdom on how to respond to the issue of engaging young teens in structured learning activities.

When listening to young teens, one begins to see that the vision for ensuring quality learning opportunities in nonschool hours must move beyond discussions of availability, access, and

NEW DIRECTIONS FOR YOUTH DEVELOPMENT, NO. 112, WINTER 2006 © WILEY PERIODICALS, INC.
Published online in Wiley InterScience (www.interscience.wiley.com) • DOI: 10.1002/yd.192

even quality. Young teens and their parents clearly stated that the "if you build it, they will come" approach, even if well built, is only part of the solution for engaging young people in learning opportunities.

In this chapter, we consider data from youth and parents about how young people spend their time, what youth and parents want from out-of-school time, and ways to creatively and organically meet the needs of families during the middle years, and we explore implications for communities and youth organizations.

What's Up? study

Interviews with young teens were conducted as part of a larger study exploring participation in structured programs in five geographically diverse communities across one midwestern state. The main goal of this study was to provide community leaders and practitioners with a better understanding of key issues and needs of youth in terms of out-of-school-time opportunities. Written surveys and individual interviews were conducted with both middle and high school students as well as parents with children in these age ranges. Most parents and youth were recruited using flyers, although some uninvolved youth were specifically targeted (for example, youth attending an alternative school). The surveys and the interviews explored participation in structured programs, perceived availability of opportunities in the community, what opportunities youth and parents wanted, and how decisions were made about what youth do when not in school.

Our findings are based on face-to-face interviews with fifty-seven youth ages 10 to 15 years (average age, 12.8 years; twenty-four girls and thirty-three boys). To provide a more complete picture, data from twenty-six parents (twenty-three mothers and three fathers) with children between the ages of 10 and 15 are also reported. Young teens and parents were not always from the same family, so the interviews were treated as independent data. Although economic and ethnic diversity was not specifically targeted in sampling, data were collected from diverse communities, including a very rural high-poverty community, an economically distressed urban neighborhood, and even alternative schools and mental health centers for youth. Those who might be considered middle class were largely from a midsized town or a suburb. The sample also included young teens and parents from new immigrant and migrant worker communities.

What youth are doing

Most of the young teens interviewed indicated that they were involved in one or more structured activities. Those involved were typically part of school sports and other extracurricular school-based activities such as band; taking private lessons in music, dance, and athletics; participating in organizations such as scouts, community education, and 4-H; and taking part in youth groups at church.

Regardless of their level of involvement, youth still reported spending a significant amount of time watching TV, playing video games, and playing on the computer. A frequent response to questions about what they did after school went something like this: "I get home, and I watch TV." Or in another case, "Lately I've been sitting around playing Gameboy. I am really good at video games. The only problem is when I get done with them, I need a new game; otherwise I get really, really bored."

Early onset of involvement

The youth in the study who were engaged in a specific activity had typically been involved since an early age. For example, one twelve-year-old girl talked about growing up in dance since the age of three and how much she loved refining her artistic movement. Others shared similar stories about the early onset of involvement where young teens found themselves skilled by their middle school years. As a result, they continued participation because they had come to enjoy it or simply because they had "grown up doing it" and had experienced success.

Given the need to feel accepted by peers, trying to find a niche in activities where other youth are already skilled and talented appears to be difficult for this age group. In fact, the ten- to fifteen-year-olds interviewed were clear that they would not try new activities at which they might not excel. "No, I am not good at that" was a frequent answer as to why they were not in other structured activities. When thrust into the harsh light of self and peer appraisal and approval, their chances for social exclusion increased if they did not conform to peer behavior or lacked talent. These concerns seemed to play a role in limiting their options for participation in available opportunities.

Role of parents

Speaking with parents about nonschool hours immediately reveals that to successfully meet the challenge of being intentional about activities for young teens, talking with youth is necessary but not sufficient. The young teens and parents interviewed agreed that parents played a critical role in getting them involved at an early age. More often than not, children ended up in activities their parents were involved in as youth ("my dad played soccer—and, well, my dad pretty much introduced me to a soccer ball, and we were just kicking it around, and then I just gradually joined a team"), or they joined groups that their parents were members of ("my mom started going to this church, like, five years ago, and as soon as I became of age, then I went to the youth group")—their parents directed them toward particular activities. In some cases, parents also directed them away from programs. When asked why he did not participate in organized activities, one boy responded, "Dad always said that I could learn just as much at home from him and doing stuff on my own than I could in organizations."

Parents interviewed also noted that they typically paid all or part of the program fees and rearranged their schedules to shuttle young teens to activities. One mother explained, "the parents have to be committed in order for them to succeed in those kinds of activities just because of the time and transportation and fundraising . . . it definitely has to be a family commitment."

NEW DIRECTIONS FOR YOUTH DEVELOPMENT • DOI: 10.1002/yd

In addition to directing their children in and out of programs at an early age, youth and parents in this study indicated that parents continued to play a significant role in making decisions about time use. For example, when asked how decisions were made about participation in activities, both parents and youth consistently reported that either parents are the sole decision makers, youth get to make their own decisions but parents still have the final say ("Mostly we ask him what he wants to do, but we have the ultimate decision"), or all decisions about activities are family decisions ("We talk about things, and usually mom and dad think things over and think what would be best for the family to do considering budgets and possibilities"). These data reveal that whether promoting or discouraging participation, parents play a critical role in what their children are doing.

Satisfaction with time use and participation in activities

It is important to note that, overall, young teens in this study were content in whatever they were doing during their nonschool hours, whether it was playing the French horn in the school band, going camping with their scout group, riding bikes, doing household chores, or watching television. There was little difference in satisfaction with time use whether youth were spending most of their time watching TV and playing video games or they were heavily involved in structured programs.

For the young teens and parents interviewed, availability and accessibility of programs seemed to be the least of their worries. What stands out in these data is that young teens and parents were in agreement on the two things that concerned them the most for this age group: to do well in school and to do well socially. Parents reported that as long as their children did well in school and had good friends, they were satisfied with how their children were spending their nonschool hours. In essence, they are not waiting for some structured opportunity in the community to fill their time, nor is there a sense of urgency to advocate for more structured programs in the community.

What youth and parents want

What involved youth want

Even though young teens expressed satisfaction with their involvement and time use, many did claim boredom and wished for more things to do. When pushed to think about what would make their nonschool hours better, most indicated that they wanted places where they could be physically active (for example, open gym, skating rink, skateboard park), do recreational activities (such as biking, fishing, swimming, arts and crafts), and have more opportunities to socialize with friends.

From the youth perspective, "hanging out with friends" keeps them active so they "don't lay around as much." For example, a thirteen-year-old boy described his typical after-schoool regimen to include doing homework, napping, and watching TV. However, over the weekend, he visited his friend to "skateboard, play football, soccer, and ride bikes." There is a widespread perception that youth spend their whole school day with friends. But youth indicated that this was not their reality. During school, they rarely find chances to visit with friends because they have separate classes, have little time between classes, are often rushed through lunch in shifts, and typically, school and out-of-school activities are based on talent and interests rather than friendship circles.

What uninvolved youth want

The uninvolved youth most consistently requested small-group, flexible, leisure, and interest-based activities. Although even uninvolved youth were generally content with what they were doing outside of school, they wanted to "do somethin' besides just sit there." The youth who were not part of a structured youth program still longed for involvement in something that stemmed from their personal interests. A twelve-year-old boy from an alternative school explained, "Sometimes I'm just sitting at home in front of the TV, and I don't really care for sitting in front of the TV like I know some people would. . . . I hate it when my friends just sit in front of a PlayStation. . . . I like arts and crafts. But we don't have [the supplies] around the house."

These youth interviewed talked about having an interest in fishing, dance, Pokemon, Star Wars, and learning a language but did not want to be part of larger programs ("I don't like those ones that are always, like, say, an organized activity, and everybody has to do that one activity, or they're boring. . ."). One fourteen-year-old boy who had never been involved in activities explained, "I don't like the people . . . sometimes they [other youth] judge you too much." He went on to say that he was not involved "Because I don't need to. Other people need to because they wanna make friends." He would prefer to go fishing and thought it would be fun to have a fishing club because "You don't usually fight with the other person when you're fishing. We could be spread out. . . . Anybody could start a conversation." The types of opportunities described by uninvolved youth do not necessarily result from a structured youth program but more often take the form of youth "hanging out" with an adult or other youth who may share their specific interests.

What parents want

Interestingly, parents interviewed agreed with the young teens when it came to what they wanted for their children. Parents reported that they wanted their children involved in structured programs so that responsible adults were supervising them, and they were simultaneously preventing the "I'm bored" syndrome. Consequently, parents could feel comfortable making the assumption that their teen was not getting into trouble. For instance, one mother said, "It keeps them occupied . . . then he's less apt to get into trouble and find other distractions that aren't as healthy." Just as important, however, parents stressed that they wanted their young teen to have the opportunity to socialize with peers. Like the young teens in the study, parents also advocated for more unstructured environments where youth could relax and visit with friends.

Although we often hear about children being overscheduled, these parents reported working to ensure that structured activities did not take up every second of the family's day. When a program did not fit the family's schedule or cut into family time, a child was not likely to participate. Youth in rural communities and urban neighborhoods reported that they lacked the time to participate because of family responsibilities. Whether helping on the farm by picking rock or walking beets (that is, weeding the fields) or babysitting younger siblings and cousins, many young teens described contributing to the family. Structured or not, many activities children were involved in became "a family activity."

Consistently, young teens and parents advocated for flexibility, less structure, and more leisure with small groups of good friends who shared a specific interest. For instance, when asked what is missing in the community, parents talked about specialized activities such as archery, sewing, or auto mechanics. However, they also realized that such customized programs were often unrealistic (because of limited resources and few youth with a particular interest), especially in smaller communities. Both young teens and parents appear resigned when it comes to the realities of what their communities can offer.

Building learning experiences

Several common threads emerged from the interviews that should challenge us to reconsider our programming strategies. By all accounts, youth and parents were content with how they were spending nonschool hours, and there was not a sense of urgency for involvement in any particular structured program. Those who are in structured programs have typically been involved since an earlier age, and the window of time to involve youth in new opportunities appears to narrow markedly by the middle school years. The young teens in the interview suggested we could reengage their interests by creating opportunities that are flexible, less structured, more leisure based, and where they could spend more time with their close friends.

Community and youth-serving organizations play a critical role in the lives of youth by building intentional learning opportunities and by encouraging positive youth development in community contexts.[1] Yet the youth most in need of these supports are often outside the programming circle.[2] Data from uninvolved youth revealed that the "structure" in structured programs may be a barrier to participation. So the question becomes, How do we merge what we know about quality learning environments with what young teens want?

Less structure and more connection

It has been established that a strong curriculum guide and a solid program plan often lead to positive learning experiences for involved youth. However, some of the most stimulating learning experiences can also emerge from the simplest conditions. We have learned from the young teens in this study that, more than anything, they want to be with their friends and perhaps connect with adults who are passionate about common interests, such as learning Spanish or planning a fishing trip. These experiences are informal and simply grow from connections that develop between youth and adults who are involved in a mutual interest.

Several youth gave a great example of a Spanish teacher at their middle school who decided to start an after-school 4-H Spanish club. Although most students had never been in 4-H, they expressed excitement at the opportunity to spend time with the popular Spanish teacher; learning and using Spanish in the communities (for example, going to a Mexican restaurant); learning conversational Spanish (less formal than the Spanish they learn at school); and to top it off, they could get extra credit points toward their grade at school. One youth talked about how he planned on helping his dad's business because many of his employees were from Mexico.

In essence, organizations need to pay particular attention to identifying those adults with special interests or hobbies who seem to have the innate ability to connect with youth. The term *wizard* is used to describe adults who possess special qualities that make them successful in working with a broad range of youth.[3] These adult wizards possess a certain way of being because they know themselves well, are deliberate in how they relate to others, and have certain assumptions about the worth of all people that filters their thoughts and feelings about others.[4] It is important to identify adults who have these qualities and connect them with young people who can benefit from the relationship.

NEW DIRECTIONS FOR YOUTH DEVELOPMENT • DOI: 10.1002/yd

Organic and free-spirited

The desired learning experiences that the young teens described have an organic element and free-spiritedness that cannot always come from a curriculum or program plan. These types of learning opportunities grow from the participants up rather than from the program down, and together youth and adults build the learning experience. These opportunities take on the energy of those involved and are shaped by personal interest. For instance, one youth said, "After school there is this girl, she is thirty-two . . . she stands outside and she brings a bunch of balls—footballs or whatever . . . and she lets a bunch of kids come over there [by the park] and play a bunch of games." Another youth described how he came to be on a skate crew: "I'm in a skate crew. We just skate and back up each other. . . . Me and my friends just started it and then started asking people if they wanted [to join] . . . we have like five or six people in it." These activities are less competitive than organized school sports, and there is not a long list of regulations to govern play. Rather, it is based on a group of people who enjoy the activity and who decide for themselves how the game will be played. These are the types of activities that a great number of youth long to become involved in, activities they can do with their friends, that are fun and recreational, with minimal structure.

Implications for communities and youth organizations

Pittman asserts that organizations should increase their efforts to reach a full range of youth needs by working in new ways.[5] Our interview data support this. Learning may occur anywhere at anytime. Organizations can help build organic learning opportunities by working with youth and adults to build learning environments like the informal environment found in pickup sports games. These organic opportunities are formed with a deliberate process that engages participants at a community level. By providing resources needed for community members to build informal learning environments in any setting, organizations can build social networks and help bring youth and adults together around diverse interests. This organic method of delivery has the potential to reach a broader range of youth.

This study reveals that communities and youth-serving organizations need to listen to young people and their parents to determine the types of learning opportunities and supports that best meet the needs of families. There is a strong desire by both youth and parents for unstructured leisure-oriented activities that connect young people to caring adults. After all, one youth noted, "you're only a kid for so long." As researchers and practitioners, we must challenge ourselves to rethink the way we frame and develop youth activities. Supervised, structured programs reach only a portion of youth some of the time. We have the responsibility to think outside of traditional program paradigms and move youth work toward a more organic process that is inclusive of a broader range of diverse needs and interests of youth and families.

Notes

1. National Research Council and Institute of Medicine, J. S. Eccles, & J. A. Gootman (Eds.). (2002). *Community programs to promote youth development. Committee on community-level programs for youth.* Washington, DC: National Academy Press.

2. Furstenberg, F. F., Cook, T. D., Eccles, J., Elder, G. H., Jr., & Sameroff, A. (1999). *Managing to make it: Urban families and adolescent success.* Chicago: University of Chicago Press; Mahoney, J. L. (2000). School extracurricular activities participation as a moderator in the development of antisocial patterns. *Child Development, 71*(2), 502–516; Mahoney, J. L., Eccles, J. S., & Larson, R. W. (2004). Processes of adjustment in organized out of school activities: Opportunities and risks. In G. G. Noam (Ed.), *After-school worlds: Creating a new social space for development and learning* (pp. 115–144). New Directions in Youth Development, no. 101. San Francisco: Jossey-Bass; Pittman, K. (1991). *Promoting youth development: Strengthening the role of youth-serving and community organizations.* Washington, DC: Academy for Educational Development.

3. McLaughlin, M. W., Irby, M. A., & Langman, J. (1994). *Urban sanctuaries: Neighborhood organizations in the lives and future of inner-city youth.* San Francisco: Jossey-Bass.

4. Skuza, J. (2005). Understanding the experiences of immigrant adolescents: Acculturation is not the same as assimilation. In P. Witt & L. Caldwell (Eds.), *Recreation and youth development.* State College, PA: Venture Publishing.
5. Pittman. (1991).

MARY S. MARCZAK *is a youth development researcher and evaluator at the Center for 4-H and Community Youth Development, University of Minnesota.*

JODI DWORKIN *is an assistant professor with the Department of Family Social Science and Extension Service at the University of Minnesota.*

JENNIFER SKUZA *is a professor and the director of the Urban 4-H Youth Development Program at the University of Minnesota.*

JANET BEYER *is an extension professor and regional educator in community youth development at the University of Minnesota.*

Working on supply and access are necessary but not sufficient for the task of increasing young people's engagement in positive youth programs, activities, and informal opportunities. Youth become the marketing experts in this endeavor to increase participation in youth programs, particularly by those who typically do not participate.

4

Beyond access and supply: Youth-led strategies to captivate young people's interest in and demand for youth programs and opportunities

Rebecca N. Saito

MOST PEOPLE WOULD PROBABLY agree that participation in quality youth programs and neighborhood-based, informal relationships and opportunities is a good thing for young people. The problem is that not nearly enough children and youth are engaged in these growth-enhancing opportunities.

Whereas estimates vary—ranging from far less than half to more than half of young people reporting that they have participated in a youth program[1]—and regardless of the actual percentage, what is clear is that there are far too many nonparticipators. This is particularly true for young teenagers: those thirteen- to fifteen-year-olds who are too old for many after-school programs and too young

NEW DIRECTIONS FOR YOUTH DEVELOPMENT, NO. 112, WINTER 2006 © WILEY PERIODICALS, INC.
Published online in Wiley InterScience (www.interscience.wiley.com) • DOI: 10.1002/yd.193

to find jobs. We see participation rates drop substantially when youth reach the middle school years.[2] This is especially troubling because these nonparticipating young teens may be particularly vulnerable to a variety of alternative competing temptations and thus, one could argue, might have the greatest need for the horizon-broadening experiences and safety nets that youth programs can provide.[3]

What can we learn from young people about designing captivating opportunities for positive youth development? And how can the unique expertise and perspectives of young people be unleashed to create effective marketing strategies to increase the interest and participation of their peers in these programs and relationships? These are the fundamental questions, the common threads that wind through the journey described in this chapter.

The journey begins with focus groups with young people in rural, suburban, and urban communities in Minnesota, then moves to two youth community-mapping projects in which young people interviewed other youth in their community. These experiences led finally to a pilot project that moves beyond issues of supply and access to a social marketing project designed by and for young people.

The journey

There are several primary sources of data from which this journey and chapter draw. The first source comes from focus groups[4] that were conducted with just over one hundred middle and high school youth ($N = 101$) in eight Minnesota towns and cities during the spring of 2004. Sites were chosen to represent a broad range of community size and type, including two rural communities (one with about 400 residents and another with about 3,000); two small towns, both between 10,000 and 20,000; two suburbs that represent two very different communities in terms of average family income and new development; and three inner-core neighborhoods in two cities with populations between 250,000 and 350,000.

NEW DIRECTIONS FOR YOUTH DEVELOPMENT • DOI: 10.1002/yd

The only criterion for participation was that the young people represent the range of youth in that community in ethnicity, family income, and participation or nonparticipation in after-school youth programs. Young people of color were intentionally overrepresented in our sample compared with state demographics, with nearly half (46 percent) of focus group participants being nonwhite. Data from these focus groups led to a typology, described later in this chapter, for categorizing communities based on the primary location and type of youth programs available in that community.

The second source of data was two parallel youth-mapping projects, one rural and one urban, that involved youth interviewing other youth in their community about the availability of youth-friendly programs, people, and places.[5] These projects provided a unique opportunity to better understand the supply side of the supply-and-demand equation from the perspective of young people in these communities.

When it comes to increasing participation in youth programs, the youth-mapping projects led to these conclusions:

• Young people often do not know what is available even in their own neighborhoods
• Young teens have far more say about how they spend their discretionary time out of school than they did when they were younger
• To actually get nonparticipating young people to come to a youth program, let alone become fully engaged in it, we need to learn from and with young people about how to market youth programs and opportunities much more effectively.

Young people themselves hold the keys to solving the participation puzzle because only they know where to find and how to talk to nonparticipators, they know what mediums to use to reach teens, and youth are in the best position to create and deliver messages and invitations to become involved. Recognizing that when it comes to social marketing as a strategy to increase participation rates, young people are experts, and a pilot project called the Youth Action Crew (YAC) was created.[6] YAC is a youth-led strategy to increase awareness of and demand for youth programs. A more in-depth discussion follows the key lessons from this journey.

The supply side: Toward a typology of youth development opportunities

In any given community, youth development opportunities—that is, relationships, experiences, and programs that promote the healthy development of young people—could theoretically occur in myriad settings and situations, including formal and nonformal programs in schools, nonprofit youth organizations, and faith institutions, as well as informal (that is, nonprogrammatic or naturally occurring) relationships and experiences. As a result of our visits and focus groups with youth in these eight very different communities, a framework was created for describing what types of youth development opportunities a community might offer its young people.

The typology described in Figure 4.1 categorizes communities by the quantity and location or type of youth development programs and opportunities that are available to young people in that community. It provides a lens for thinking about and assessing the extent to which a community provides the opportunities for growth that young people need.

Ideally, a community that is rich in opportunity offers a comprehensive array of high-quality accessible programs in schools and in the broader community and surrounds young people with caring, involved neighbors, businesses, and other organizations. Our analysis of the focus group data revealed no opportunity-rich communities in which school-, community-, and faith-based activities were prevalent and complemented by informal supports. According to the young people who participated in the study, communities were either school-based opportunity rich or opportunity depleted. In no community were positive informal nonprogrammatic supports or opportunities cited as common or adequate.

NEW DIRECTIONS FOR YOUTH DEVELOPMENT • DOI: 10.1002/yd

Figure 4.1. Three types of communities based on the quality and predominant type of youth development opportunities

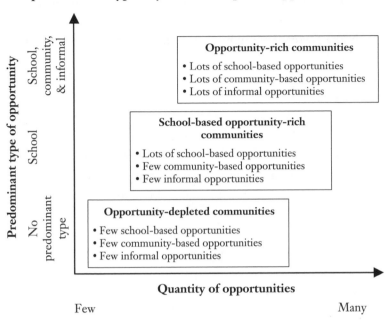

Small townships (populations less than one thousand) and large urban centers appear to share some similarities in terms of this typology. In both types of communities, the ratio of the number of programs to the number of children and youth appears to be low, and access to school- or community-based activities was reported to be limited because of both transportation issues and cost. In contrast, somewhat larger but still rural towns (more than three thousand) and suburbs seem more likely to have school-based after-school opportunities available to them, though relatively few community-based programs and informal relationships.

Previous studies of Minneapolis[7] suggest that there are pockets of the city with many community- and school-based activities for certain age groups (especially for elementary school children), whereas in other neighborhoods there are almost none. In no neighborhood, however, are there nearly enough options to accommodate the sheer number of youth and their varied interests.

NEW DIRECTIONS FOR YOUTH DEVELOPMENT • DOI: 10.1002/yd

Formal programs

The location and type of youth development opportunities (whether school, community, or faith based) that are available to youth in a particular community are important because each may attract different kinds of youth, provide different benefits, and have differing levels of access and support, according to focus group participants.

Generally, young people said that community-based programs do or should allow youth to explore a broader range of interests and experiences than school-based programs but that they also require more initiative on the part of the young person to find out what is available and to make the effort to get and stay involved. School-based programs, on the other hand, are more likely to have built-in supports and motivational factors that affect participation—for example, earning public recognition, late-activity buses, or seeing program staff on premises for school-based programs. However, young people said that school-based activities might be less attractive to students who are not doing well academically. In particular, youth talked about the differences between school-based and community-based programs in these ways:

You get a different feeling in school-based activities. Like, with school softball, you get school pride, but with nonschool softball, I'm doing my passion.

There is a different kind of engagement in nonschool activities because being less structured allows you to take initiative and make choices and different friends.

It's more challenging to be in nonschool-related activities because it gives you the chance to think and be separate from the identity you have in school. It also takes more motivation to be in nonschool activities because the structure, the consequences, the school-related motivational factors—like teachers seeing you throughout the day—are not there.

Young people's perspectives on school-based and community-based youth programs are compared in Table 4.1.

NEW DIRECTIONS FOR YOUTH DEVELOPMENT • DOI: 10.1002/yd

Table 4.1. School-based versus community-based youth development opportunities from the perspective of youth

Characteristic	School based	Community based
Structure	Activity tends to be more structured	Activity tends to be less structured
Supports and incentives	External supports and motivational factors: easier to join because it is more convenient and familiar	Internal motivation: young person must be motivated to seek out opportunities
Transportation	Easier to coordinate transportation issues	Difficult to deal with transportation issues
Cost	Tend to cost more, especially sports	Tend to cost little or nothing
Perceived outcomes	School pride	Personal fulfillment; new people, places, experiences, and opportunities

Informal opportunities and relationships

In this typology, informal youth development opportunities include such things as neighbors getting involved with the youth in their neighborhood as well as youth-friendly businesses and community organizations. Somewhere on the continuum of formal to informal lie places in which young people can go to "hang out" and relax without being on task. Youth talked about informal opportunities in these ways:

My dad said he would let people build a skateboard park on his property with the extra lumber he has from a building project if he could get some help.

A lot of businesses are not youth friendly. They have rules about how many kids can be in a store at one time, and so forth. They think all kids are going to steal things or wreck stuff.

Have a supervisor available to staff the school building after hours to offer stuff like open gym, movie nights, etc., since it is the best alternative to a separate rec center.

NEW DIRECTIONS FOR YOUTH DEVELOPMENT • DOI: 10.1002/yd

Like, I always wanted to go golfing, but there aren't courses around where kids can go and golf, and no one will take me.

Programming for teens

Another dimension of the after-school youth program landscape is the distribution of programs for different age groups. In general, the number of programs available for young teenagers (thirteen- to fifteen-year-olds) compared with those available for elementary students appears to drop substantially. The exception is school sports and other school-based clubs and activities where new opportunities become available in middle and high school but only to those who are interested in the sport or activity, are good enough to make the team or squad, and can afford the activity fees.

In summary, when we think about the opportunities—and missed opportunities—for young people in any community to continue learning and growing outside the regular school day, we should think about the programs, relationships, experiences, and opportunities that could be available throughout the community, including programs in and out of schools, and nonprogrammatic, informally occurring relationships and experiences in neighborhoods.

The typology provides a framework that enables a community to assess and hopefully work to enhance the "supply side" of the equation. But paying attention to supply is not enough. We need to learn more about the demand side, that is, the needs, wishes, interests, and motivations of young people—the customers in this sense—particularly those who do not already typically participate.

Understanding and igniting demand

Regardless of community type, clearly there is much work to be done on the supply side to enhance the availability, richness, and diversity of youth development opportunities. But what do we know about the demand part of the equation? Although there may be some debate among youth programs about who their real customer is—participants, parents, or those who fund their programs—the reality is that as children mature into the middle school years, they are likely to have more say about where or even whether to participate in youth programs. In this sense, as youth reach preadolescence and early adolescence and make more decisions about how and where they spend their discretionary time, teens themselves increasingly become the customers that program providers must satisfy. Yet, as indicated previously, findings suggest that as age increases, participation in after-school programs decreases.[8]

What do these young customers want in terms of people, programs, and places to grow? How could programming and marketing or recruitment strategies change to attract these older youth? What would make it more likely that those who do not typically participate become engaged in these youth development opportunities? These are the questions that guide our examination of the demand side of youth development opportunities and programs.

Participation, nonparticipation, and characteristics of attractive young teen programming

National estimates of the percentage of youth that participate in youth programs vary greatly.[9] Nonetheless, in an earlier study of Minneapolis children and youth,[10] overall about half of young people (49 percent) reported participating in at least one youth program a week, although this varied substantially by ethnicity, neighborhood, and family income. Results from a more recent study of youth engagement opportunities in three small communities in greater Minnesota and several inner-core neighborhoods in Minneapolis[11] show participation (that is, those who have ever participated in a youth program) ranging from about 39 percent in Minneapolis to 67 percent in greater Minnesota.

Regardless of the actual percentage of youth that are engaged in youth development programs and opportunities in a specific community at a particular point in time, these data suggest that at least in Minnesota, somewhere around 30 to 60 percent of youth typically do not participate in any youth development opportunities. And that is far too many.

Why youth do not participate

There are many reasons why young people do not participate. In some communities and for many youth, there simply are not many formal programs or informal opportunities available to them (opportunity-depleted communities). But even in communities where some level of programming exists, far too many youth are not engaged in these growth-enhancing youth development opportunities.

Focus group participants listed several barriers to participation, including:

- Restricted access, including cost and transportation
- Youth feel unwelcome by adult staff or uncomfortable with other participants
- Lack of knowledge or interest in what is available to them
- The program is run poorly

Access. A program is accessible if you can afford it and can get to it. So, if you are a student who likes to participate in traditional extracurricular activities and there is a late-activity bus, then you are in luck (assuming the bus stops in your neighborhood). If, however, there is no late bus—as was the case in most of the school districts from which we drew focus group participants—and you do not have another means of transportation, then it is far less likely that you will be able to participate in any youth program, school based or otherwise. Furthermore, we learned that in some schools late-activity buses are reserved for youth who participate in only certain activities (usually mainstream sports) and are not available to youth who participate in other school-based or community-based after-school programs.

In some communities, particularly small towns and urban communities, youth often live far from their school, sometimes twenty to twenty-five miles away, and have no means of transportation outside of the one school bus that leaves right after school is done, effectively preventing them from participating in anything that is not close to their home neighborhood. It seemed that transportation was less of an issue for youth who lived in midsized towns where the school was relatively close or in suburbs where transportation seemed more readily accessible. Young people also cited cost as a barrier, particularly to participate in sports, which are likely to charge an activity fee.

Basically, if your family has money to pay for the cost of participating in programs and someone to drive you to and from various activities, then you have good access. If your family does not have money to pay various fees or cannot provide transportation, then you are probably out of luck.

Youth feel unwelcome. Beyond the issue of access was the question of social climate: whether or not young people felt welcomed and comfortable in after-school settings. A disturbing number of young people in this study talked about feeling like outsiders, that they were unwelcome or that the staff did not like them. In their words:

There are a lot of cliques, and that makes participating uncomfortable. I just don't want to be in it. In a small town, everyone knows your business, and they judge you because of your family or your brothers and sisters.

Like, there's always supervision here; they're really strict, always people watching us, like they don't trust us.

Change the staff to be nice. Get staff that talks to you in a good way. Respect you.

Lack of interest in and knowledge about what is available. One of the ironies of youth development programs (that by their nature are supposed to help youth make smart choices and be better leaders in their community) is that, for the most part, adults decide what programs to create. One of the strategies that were suggested in almost every focus group was to start with young people's interests and then develop programs based on what they like to do. Remarkably, there appear to be relatively few after-school youth development opportunities for young people to explore their own interests. Some youth mentioned small school-based grants for young people to start their own clubs, but they have to be school based and thus do not necessarily reach the low participator. There is also the Tiger Woods Foundation's Start Something, which invites young people to apply for small grants after completing a ten-session program designed to help participants achieve a goal or dream.

Lack of knowledge about what is available is another barrier to participation that is disturbing both because it is cited so frequently and because it is something we ought to be able to overcome. Advertising and marketing to teenagers is something professionals know how to do. Why do we not utilize their expertise in combination with the unique "insider" perspectives and expertise of young people and transfer this to our work in the field of out-of-school time?

A recent example of a project that is attempting to address this marketing niche is the YAC project referred to earlier. YAC is a youth-led strategy to increase participation rates in youth programs by creating a neighborhood map (Exhibit 4.1) of all the youth development programs and informal places in a community. YAC members then disseminate the free maps through a variety of targeted marketing strategies.

Quality programming

A common thread throughout these data regarding quality programming for preteens and early teens was the need to create programming that recognizes this age group's unique developmental need to have increasing levels of autonomy and authority in the design and implementation of their program or project. From the perspective of young people, quality means safe places where they can hang out with their friends and do cool things and where they can be involved in leadership opportunities and decision making, have new experiences, and develop caring, respectful relationships with other young people and adults. Further, they want to know that their opinions matter and that they can effect real change.

Caring about, being invested in, and having a stake in the success of a program increases individuals' motivation to participate

Exhibit 4.1. An example of a youth-led marketing tool designed to increase participation in youth programs

fully, which in turn reinforces commitment and ownership. From the operational side, good programs work effectively toward something, have goals that are attractive to young people, and are organized and supportive enough to accomplish the goals.

NEW DIRECTIONS FOR YOUTH DEVELOPMENT • DOI: 10.1002/yd

This is what young people said about creating programs based on their own age-appropriate interests and skills:

If you give a person a sense of purpose, give them a voice, then they'll participate.

You don't usually want to listen to adults tell you how to have fun.

Programs have to be more productive, be more relevant to our own community.

There's always someone to push you, to support you and help you reach your goals.

It would be the coolest of cool to start our own program.

I'd like to start something with people my own age. Sometimes I crave a place to talk to my peers about, I don't know, world affairs and politics, literature, current events–whatever! Like a philosopher's coffee shop or something like that.

Conversely, poor quality, from the perspective of young people, included such things as:

- The program is disorganized, chaotic, does not accomplish anything. For example, youth said things like:

I'll leave a program if it's wasting time, if I'm not learning anything.

Way too many kids, and way too wild.

It's not meaningful. Like, um, it isn't going the way you want it to go. Like, we planned a meeting and nobody showed up, just a few people.

- Youth are given no authority or responsibility and thus have little investment in the program:

We aren't brought onto this earth to do things into which we cannot put our hearts.

- Negative staff characteristics:

If people in charge underestimate us; if they're condescending.

Too much talking at us by leaders.

NEW DIRECTIONS FOR YOUTH DEVELOPMENT • DOI: 10.1002/yd

Reflections on the journey

The young people who participated in the focus groups, community mapping projects, and the YACs have taught us a great deal about engaging young people. Their insights have taken us from simply assessing what is available to a deeper understanding of why young people do not participate and what needs to be done to increase participation in captivating youth development opportunities. These forays into the issues surrounding low participation in youth development programs and opportunities at the community level have led to several key observations and recommendations.

Assess supply to identify gaps

Communities differ in the number, type, content, and settings (for instance, school versus community based) of youth development programs and opportunities that are available to their young people, and different settings may attract different kinds of young people, have different supports and barriers, and may attend to different outcomes, according to young people in Minnesota communities. Therefore, communities (and small towns, big cities, even whole states) need a way to assess supply to identify gaps in what is available.[12]

After a community learns what types of programming and other opportunities are available for their young people, it can then develop strategies to diversify and strengthen program options and work to increase access and reduce barriers to participation working with the youth themselves.

Young teens may need these opportunities the most but participate the least

It appears that the supply of and participation in community-based programming decrease as age increases. This is particularly troubling because it is precisely these youth who are developmentally ready to receive support from people outside the home and need the caring relationships, safe places, new opportunities, and attention to a variety of social and academic outcomes that youth programs can provide.

Programming for teens requires a different approach

We need to understand that programming for teenagers is different from that for younger participants. For preteens and teens, it is about developing programs and opportunities with them, not for them. Young people said they enjoy working experientially in project-based models in which they have some level of autonomy and influence over important decisions, they have a strong desire to make a difference in their community and effect real change, and they want to be treated with respect by staff and other participants and viewed as resources in their community.

As children move into their second decade of life, they have different interests and needs and growing influence over decisions about how they spend their discretionary time outside of school. As a result of these developmental shifts, program providers, youth worker training institutions, and policymakers need to change the content of programs and opportunities to match the interests of teenagers and provide training for youth workers to be facilitators of young people's growth and development, not didactic instructors or child care providers.

Attending to the supply side is necessary but not sufficient

Addressing supply issues by creating more opportunities for youth development is absolutely essential, but increasing supply alone may not be enough to reach the goal of increasing the percentage of youth who are engaged in programs and their community. For the field of after-school programming, the old adage, "Build it and they will come," does not necessarily apply, at least with regard to youth in the middle years.

Increase demand through youth-led marketing strategies

As a field of study, we need to create ways of reaching and marketing directly to teens to encourage higher levels of participation. The YAC is one example of a youth-led marketing strategy to increase participation, but we need to learn more about effective ways to reach these young people.

The power of youth as customers, market researchers, and change agents

What we learn from these data is that we need to shift our orientation from thinking of teenagers as children and recipients of service to seeing them as young adults with the power to choose what they will do with their leisure time and as resources and leaders who, if given the right supports and opportunities to succeed, will meet and exceed our expectations.

We need to develop programs in partnership with young people that will be captivating to this diverse audience. We need to use the unique expertise of young people in creating effective marketing strategies, especially with regard to reaching youth who typically do not participate in youth programs.

As a nation, we have brought attention, policies, and funding to the needs of prenatal care and early childhood. We have begun to acknowledge the need for and federally fund after-school programming for elementary school children. Let us continue up the developmental ladder to recognize the unique needs and strengths of adolescents and work to ensure that their voices are heard in this call to action.

Notes

1. Eccles, J. S., & Gootman, J. A. (Eds.). (2002). *Community programs to promote youth development: Committee on community-level programs for youth.* Washington, DC: National Academy Press.

2. Wilson-Ahlstrom, A., Yohalem, N., & Pittman, K. (2003). *Participation during out-of-school time: Taking a closer look.* Out-of-School-Time Policy Commentary no. 6. Washington, DC: Forum for Youth Investment.

3. Lauver, S., Little, P., & Weiss, H. (2004). *Moving beyond the barriers: Attracting and sustaining youth participation in out-of-school-time programs.* Issues and Opportunities in Out-of-School-Time Evaluation, no. 6. Cambridge, MA: Harvard Family Research Project.

4. Saito, R. N. (2005). *Listening to young people's voices on out-of-school-time opportunities.* Brief written for the Minnesota Commission on Out-of-School Time. http:/www.mncost.org/YouthVoices.pdf

5. Calhoun, R. D., & Saito, R. N. (2005). *The Howland road trip: A journey from research to practice.* Keynote address themes for Howland Symposium on DVD format, University of Minnesota, Minneapolis.

6. The Youth Action Crew is a joint project of the Minneapolis Youth Coordinating Board, YO! The Movement, and the Center for 4-H and Community Youth Development at the University of Minnesota.

7. Saito, R. N., Benson, P. L., Blyth, D. A., & Sharma, A. R. (1995). *Places to grow: Perspectives on youth development opportunities for seven- to 14-year-old Minneapolis youth*. Minneapolis: Search Institute.

8. Wilson-Ahlstrom et al. (2003).

9. Eccles and Gootman. (2002).

10. Saito et al. (1995).

11. Calhoun and Saito. (2005).

12. Quinn, J. (1999, Fall). Where need meets opportunity: Youth development programs for early teens. *Future of Children: When School Is Out*, *9*(2), 96–116.

REBECCA N. SAITO *is a senior fellow at the Center for 4-H and Community Youth Development at the University of Minnesota and an independent consultant in the area of neighborhood-based youth development.*

Intentionality, including a lived ethos of positive youth development, is the key to success in engaging young people in out-of-school learning experiences that meet their developmental needs and everyday interests.

5

Intentional youth programs: Taking theory to practice

Joyce A. Walker

ALMOST ANY YOUTH PROGRAM has the potential to be hollow busywork or a vibrant learning experience. Research has documented important features of supportive environments,[1] choice and flexibility,[2] balancing youth and adult-driven stances,[3] and the centrality of relationships.[4] The challenge for practitioners is to construct and carry out youth development programs in ways that incorporate the lessons of research as well as get young people in the door and actively engaged. In this chapter, I present a conceptual program development framework based on the theory of developmental intentionality.[5] Through examples from research and practice, I attempt to "make real" the abstract theory so that it has application for daily work. The framework illustrates how a program carefully grounded in a youth development ethos and a deliberately designed learning experience model creates opportunities that engage and are a good fit for youth in the middle years.

The first section of this chapter focuses on a theory and a framework for actualizing the theory. A short explanation of the theory

NEW DIRECTIONS FOR YOUTH DEVELOPMENT, NO. 112, WINTER 2006 © WILEY PERIODICALS, INC.
Published online in Wiley InterScience (www.interscience.wiley.com) • DOI: 10.1002/yd.194

of developmental intentionality includes a discussion of how intentionality, engagement, and goodness of fit come together to energize a youth program and help it achieve its intended outcomes. Next, a discussion of the framework for a developmentally intentional program moves the theory into practical application. The elements of the framework are an ethos of youth development, a model for designing a learning experience, and the presence of young people in the context of their everyday life. The second section of the chapter describes actual community-based programs for early adolescents. Experienced practitioners selected these programs because they illustrate ways to achieve engagement and goodness of fit through deliberate program strategies. The chapter concludes with a series of important questions that encourage practitioners to scrutinize their programs and practices through the lens of intentionality, thus providing a frame for what one prioritizes, what one decides to do, and how one evaluates the effort.

Theory of developmental intentionality

The theory of developmental intentionality begins with the belief that young people such as those in the middle years are more likely to achieve desired developmental outcomes when they are actively engaged in their own learning and development. The theory proposes that when there is a good fit between young people and the intentional supports and opportunities they take part in, engagement is high, and the chances of positive outcomes for learning and development are greatly improved. *Engagement* speaks to the extent to which young people are involved, interested, and enthusiastic about what they are doing. Engagement can reflect deep interest in a particular activity or involvement over time in a larger learning experience. *Goodness of fit* refers to a positive synergy between the needs and nature of a young person and the supports and opportunities present in the program. On one level, goodness of fit is a result of engagement in intentional experiences; likewise, learning experiences can be intentionally designed to promote goodness of fit with individual youth, resulting in high levels of engagement and increased chances of good developmental outcomes.

NEW DIRECTIONS FOR YOUTH DEVELOPMENT • DOI: 10.1002/yd

Framework for a developmentally intentional program

Since the introduction of the theory of developmental intentionality in the design of youth programs, practitioners and scholars have resonated to the visual representation of a young person engaging in an intentional program (Figure 5.1).

Represented in the figure are the framework elements for a developmentally intentional youth program. Implementation of the theory requires first of all an operational ethos of youth development, a philosophy and way of working with young people that permeates the program and, ideally, the organization. The visual

Figure 5.1. Framework for developmentally intentional youth program

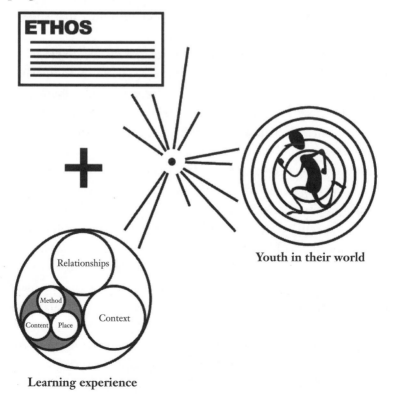

ETHOS

Youth in their world

Relationships

Method

Content Place Context

Learning experience

image for the ethos is a box filled with accepted youth development principles and practices. Second, the theory requires an intentional model for the learning experience (also referred to as the program). The visual image of circles within circles represents the multiple aspects of a program. Each circle represents a major program component. The effect is to allow the program leader to deliberately adjust various aspects of the learning experience to achieve the desired outcomes, such as creating a better fit with the needs of the young people, executing more effective processes for learning, or substituting different content to generate deeper levels of engagement. Last, there is no program without young people who come and participate. The visual image of a young person is superimposed on the concentric circles associated with Bronfenbrenner's ecological model of human development.[6] It is a reminder that youth are at the center of youth development work, and they come to programs bringing their worlds along with them to be incorporated into the experience as one aspect of engagement and good fit.

This theory and program framework suggest that youth programs stimulate engagement and good fit—the splash in the middle—when they live out a vibrant, inclusive spirit and a positive, just philosophy, referred to here as an ethos of youth development. Equally important, the content and design of youth programs are shaped in intentional ways to build relationships, to be responsive to the everyday context of young people's lives, and to create developmentally appropriate learning experiences with and on behalf of young people. Quality program activities depend on a deliberate blend of relevant, interesting content; appropriate pedagogy; and a safe, stimulating environment. The bottom line is that both the philosophy or ethos and the deliberate design of a program require special attention.

Intentionality is like an intervention that stimulates engagement and strengthens the goodness of fit between the youth and program, thus increasing the chances of achieving desired learning and developmental outcomes. The term "developmental intentionality" is used to describe this type of purposeful intervention. The term "program," as used here, means a deliberately constructed learning experience for young people. This could be a week at camp, a season of soccer, a daylong field trip, or a nine-month club experience. Because the philosophy and design of youth programs require special attention to achieve engagement and good fit, a larger discussion of ethos, youth in their everyday life context, and learning experiences is useful.

Youth development ethos

Adults who work with young people benefit personally and professionally from a clear, strong commitment to a philosophy of youth development that guides their everyday work. When this way of thinking is actualized as a way of working daily with peers and youth, a spirit or ethos of respect, inclusion, and possibility becomes obvious to everyone around the program. Young people are attracted to this proactive, inviting spirit of youth development. Fundamental to a youth development ethos is a commitment to six principles that have emerged from scholarship in the field:

- *Build on basic youth needs.* Young people in the middle years need to feel a sense of safety and structure and to experience active participation, membership, and belonging. They need to develop self-worth through meaningful contribution and to experiment to discover self. It is equally important to develop significant quality relationships with peers and adults, discuss conflicting values and form their own, feel the pride of competence and mastery, and expand their capacity to enjoy life and know that success is possible.[7]
- *Provide choice and flexibility.* Young people are more likely to take charge of their own learning and development when voluntary opportunities offer young people developmentally appropriate choices regarding their level of participation, their leadership roles, and their ways of contributing.[8]
- *Create together.* Active cocreation between youth and adults establishes shared leadership and shared power. Youth-adult partnerships encourage valuing and inclusion of the talents of young

and old and truly allow young people to be active instruments of their own learning and development.

- *Situate learning in everyday life.* Living and learning are not separate, and learning experiences that promote real work, service learning, and contributions to family and community resonate with youth in the middle years.

- *Embrace an asset-based approach.* Emphasize what is positive about young people rather than what is wrong with them. This fosters building strengths, creating opportunities, offering supports, and rewarding signs of healthy development.

- *Commit to a cohesive approach to learning.* Responsive programs that address youth development outcomes broadly have demonstrated a higher level of effectiveness than approaches that targeted specific behaviors or skills to avoid specific behaviors.[9]

An example illustrating the power of a strong ethos is found in Art First,[10] where Larson and Walker found adults who were driven by their ethos of respect, caring, and positive development to go the extra mile as they made program decisions for the good of youth involved. In one case, students in a summer arts program completed personal representational murals designed as public art only to have their efforts vandalized within days of being installed in a community setting. The staff felt devastated, and the young people were angry and disillusioned. The summer program would have ended on this sad note of failure if staff had not responded creatively out of their commitment to the young people. When they offered to hold new classes on art restoration so that the young people could learn the skills necessary to right the wrong that had been done, the youth responded enthusiastically. A spirit of resilience, grounded in a belief in young people and in the pursuit of a just resolution, moved the adults and youth to work together to recreate the murals, an affirmation for themselves and the community. Their intentional actions reflected their value for the artistic process, their pride in artistic products, and their respect for their artists. With this ethos at work, the plan to have youth restore their work made perfect sense.

Embracing youth in the context of their everyday lives

The young people coming to youth programs bring all the values, experiences, customs, culture, assets, and deficits of their developmental ecology: their life stories; their families, neighborhoods, and schools; and the larger city, state, and nation in which they live. They come to build on their strengths with needs to be addressed, interests to be explored, and assets of all sorts to contribute. They are full of possibility, energy, and challenges. Young people want to be welcomed and respected for all that they are, not approached or treated as neutral beings absent their larger ecology. Knowing and embracing the fullness of young people are critical to stimulating engagement and determining a good developmental fit for each person.

· In her research with Somali girls, Bigelow[11] provides an example of how learning experiences without intentional strategies to promote and prepare through activities that invite stories, promote cultural sharing, search out arenas for youth contribution, and actively stimulate engagement may permit a young person to sink into the background, become an observer, and potentially drop out. Bigelow describes how the resilience, strength, and powerful assets of a young immigrant woman, "Fadumo" (not her real name), were interpreted and labeled as problems by the adults around her. Instead of building on the responsibilities and influence she played in her family and trying to understand the issues inherent in being a sixteen-year-old girl attending the first school in her life, adults responded in deficit terms. They made few demands in the classroom, rewarded compliant behavior, and complained that she did not stay after school for supplemental help. Without an intentional plan to do otherwise, no one inquired about her life before coming to America, so no one realized that her family had spent six years in a refugee camp where her mother taught the children to read and inspired them with a love of the rich oral folktale tradition of their culture.

How different it would be if an adult had taken the time to learn about Fadumo's family, her life, and her leadership. She supervised younger family members after school, prepared meals, and tutored younger siblings in homework tasks each evening. Her life

trajectory was unfamiliar, so it was labeled, perhaps unintention-
ally, as negative. In a community-based youth program where the
researcher met Fadumo, her talents were a great asset. She was
encouraged to share her rich experiences—her social and cultural
capital—with other youth, and she tapped her deep funds of knowledge to contribute to her friends and the community.

Learning experience model

The learning experience model makes responsiveness to relationships,
community context, and the quality of activities a priority. Indeed,
these are the three larger circles in the visual model (Figure 5.1). Program leaders usually have responsibility for determining the youth
development outcomes of the program. Some do this alone, some
in consultation with colleagues. Others actively involve youth in
the process. The success of these desired outcomes depends on the
degree to which the program intentionally promotes them. Every
outcome carries implications for the guiding ethos, the young people, and the shape of the learning experiences. In every case, healthy,
caring, respectful relationships between adults and youth are critical.
This can mean firmly established boundaries or negotiated ones,
depending on the program goals and outcomes. Staff and program
responsiveness to the values, culture, and context of the youth, families, and community builds success. This connection also makes the
achievements more valuable to young people because they are visibly
valuable to others they care about. Stimulating, well-planned activities
that allow youth to enter and participate at levels appropriate to them
individually are the main attraction. It is in this area of the learning
experience that most program efforts and resources are focused: the
place, the content of activities, the methods of teaching and learning.

· The Whitman Action Crew[12] is an example of a community-
based research project intentionally structured to engage neighborhood youth too young to drive in solving a community
problem.[13] The decision by youth and adults to map a ten-square-
block urban neighborhood to identify youth-friendly places was a
response to data showing that close to 65 percent of their peers did
not know about youth activities or structured programs in their

neighborhood. The adult leaders identified funding for stipends and put out an invitation for youth to join them in mapping and then marketing the programs in their community. Attention to relationships, responsiveness to community concerns, and careful forethought to all activities—those three large circles in the model—were hallmarks of their work together. As a team, the adults and youth worked to intentionally develop relationships with each other as they gathered each day for lunch together, shared their lives, set their goals, and made their plans. As a group, they decided how to approach the work, make a plan, and get the job done. There was a lot of purposeful learning. They gained the skills to decipher census data and interview agency staff. They came to trust and admire each other. They learned about programs and systematically spread the word to families in a door-to-door marketing campaign. The stipends ran out, and the youth kept working. They published a map of youth-friendly places, posted signs proclaiming "Youth Are Here!" in front of program sites, and even told the city mayor and police chief about their experience. Cocreating, meeting basic youth needs, grounding learning in everyday community needs, having fun and making a difference: these are all good program practices driven by a shared ethos of inclusion, respect, and commitment to building individual and community assets.

Intentional strategies for intentional practice with early adolescents

The program descriptions and recommendations that follow are shared by three reflective professionals with extensive experience with youth programs and research involving youth in the middle years.[14] One, a foundation program officer with a portfolio of over one hundred youth programs, uses research and practical wisdom gained over many years to fund intentional strategies that successfully engage youth in the middle years. The other two, a program director at a large urban community agency and an experienced researcher and consultant, partnered to share a university-endowed chair for a year.[15] In that role, they studied effective bridging strategies between university research and community practice as they worked with youth in the nine-to-fifteen-year age group who did not participate in youth programs and with informal asset builders supporting young people in the community.

Figure 5.2 illustrates the integration of the ethos, learning experience, and young person in a developmentally intentional program. The emphasis here is on engagement and good fit, with the suggestion of positive energy among the three elements of the framework. The program examples that follow were shared by the three thoughtful practitioners because they contain intentional strategies to create a synergy between the ethos, the learning experience, and the young person to generate engagement and goodness of fit. In

Figure 5.2. A developmentally intentional program

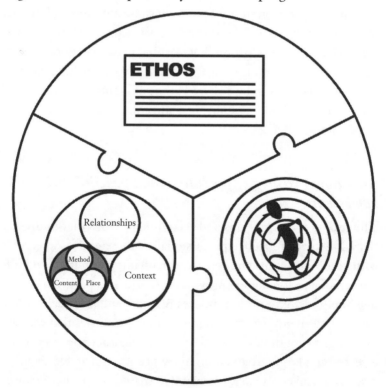

addition, the examples illustrate, in the minds of the practitioners, important features of quality programs for early adolescents. Although these programs have not been evaluated in terms of the framework for developmentally intentional programs, they are programs that stand out and are recognized and valued in the community. They have many years of longevity, a broad base of parent and community support, a reasonably stable funding base, experienced staff, and a large base of young people who keep coming year after year, often bringing their siblings with them.

Ethos transparency

The experienced practitioners agreed that a clear youth development ethos is a source of energy for staff and youth. Professionals and programs benefit when they boldly identify who they are and what they stand for. Young people have a good nose for authenticity and quality.[16] Agencies committed to youth and adult partnerships do well to identify the many ways youth have voice in determining the program direction because this has appeal to youth in the middle years. Places dedicated to learning do well to describe the kind of choices available and the progression of opportunities available for youth who are ready to move ahead. Articulation of the ethos can be effectively reinforced in many ways, such as in visual art, marketing materials, signs of respect for young people, and clear ground rules and program values posted for all to see.

Youth farmers' market. Our wise informants praised programs infused with expanding opportunities at every step. Such programs allow youth to join and stay for several years because they have opportunities for progressive learning and leadership. Youth stay because they want to be there; their parents encourage this because they know the staff and trust the program. Our program officer noted that youth in the middle years often express fears about joining new groups and reluctance about trying new things in unfamiliar environments. She encourages intentional efforts to keep this middle age group in programs they already know and like. At the youth farmers' market, young people can wash spinach, harvest spinach, plant spinach, sell spinach, market spinach to restaurants, deliver spinach, and eventually supervise the younger kids in the farm and market business. There are seasonal cycles, but the program is year-round, an important feature noted by the experts who see the value in maintaining youth-adult contact and relationships throughout the year. The ethos driving this program values continuity and belonging as well as progressively expanding chances to take on new responsibilities and master new skills. The values of fresh food, good nutrition, leadership, and rites of passage seem to resonate with youth in the middle years, who report liking the clear expectations, the consistent staff, and the chance to try new things.

Intentionality in all things

No program can do everything, but it is important to be intentional about what is done and what is not done. It is not uncommon for the activities—the content, the learning methods, and the environment—to be the first (and perhaps only) aspect of the program that gets attention. Sometimes in the short term, activities trump other aspects of the program, but in the long term a balance is important. Deliberate attention to relationships and to the cultural and community context of the young people is as significant as the activities young people take part in. The learning experience is most fully developed when it intentionally considers all aspects of the model. The reflective practitioners cite these examples of how relationships, responsiveness to context, and quality activities were hallmarks of quality programs.

Henry and Iris. Relationships are central, and they extend beyond the youth and staff in a program. Believing that many urban neighborhoods had strong informal networks of neighbors and businesses that supported young people, our wise urban program director spent a year systematically studying the role of informal community-asset builders in the lives of youth in the middle years. Young people taught him about Henry and Iris. This older couple, like many others in the community, invited young people into their lives. Trusted by families and youth alike, they served up food, soul, and advice about everything from prom dresses to homework. They listened to stories of part-time jobs, hobbies, troubles at school, and aspirations for the future. Like the man who organizes pickup baseball at the park Sunday afternoons and the fellow who opens his garage for fixing bicycles, these adults offered voluntary friendships that mattered to young people. Our director observed that strong programs intentionally nurture connections with the community's informal asset builders to the benefit of youth and their programs. Although informal asset builders are not volunteers in the traditional sense of people with agency job descriptions, they are community champions, helpers, and advisors who make themselves available to youth right where they are just because they like them. Although all relationships deserve attention—adult-adult, adult-youth, youth-youth—the informal asset-builder relationships reach beyond the boundaries of program and draw on essential community talent and support that in turn makes programs even stronger.

YouthRESPOND. Responsiveness to community context is a priority for YouthRESPOND. This program exemplifies deliberate efforts to work intensively year-round to respond to the concerns and interests of the youth, communities, and families they serve. They dig deep into issues of cultural context and positive relationships. The program began as a summer camp for urban kids and has grown into a multicultural youth employment and leadership program that builds relationships and sustains them all year-round. The emphasis on preemployment skills and opportunities for real work draw youth in. In response to youth needs and interests, YouthRESPOND follows their residential camp season with myriad opportunities for mentoring, weekend trips, weekly activities, community service, retreats, and employment opportunities. Youth leadership opportunities and experiences with conflict resolution are just two of the ways young people come together, bridging the divides of culture, neighborhood, and school boundaries. It is all about fostering multicultural awareness in safe and fun environments, a high-demand focus in a metropolitan area rich in the diversity of new immigrant as well as traditional cultures.

Soul Academy. Activities at Soul Academy draw deeply on the larger cultural context of youth and their families in the community.

To achieve its mission to educate, empower, and engage youth ages eleven to fourteen years to build positive futures, this program chooses program content, learning methods, and a learning environment trusted and accepted by the African American community it serves. The focus on social change reflects community priorities, and young people put hip-hop to use in action-and-change projects that they select and work on. Building community is also a priority because Soul Academy and its companion programs focus on a middle school where 97 percent of students receive free or reduced lunches, 40 percent are classified as homeless or highly mobile, and there are no after-school activities. In creating a web of support for the families and young people involved, this program combines a strong youth development ethos with intentional activities, relationships, and responsiveness to community context.

Activities draw youth

All three practitioners emphasized the role of developmentally appropriate activities in engaging youth in the middle years. Initially young people come for the activities and the other friends who participate. And although kids this age cannot drive, they can walk away when they lose interest or have a bad experience. Relationships may be the ultimate essential element of a good youth program, but a good reputation, a warm invitation, and a menu of attractive activities generally draw youth in the door.

Engaging activities demand attention to content, method, and environment. The key concepts mentioned were age-appropriate, youth-selected content; hands-on, active learning methods; and out-of-the-box, out-of-the-building spaces that connect youth to the real world of community. Our experts particularly mentioned opportunities for skill building and practice that leads to mastery. Youth in the middle years are ripe to put what they know into practice and to practice what they know till they get it right. When these learning opportunities have a sequence, continuity, and integration with each other and the real world, they meet long-accepted criteria for good curriculum.[17]

Apply the lens of developmental intentionality to practice

In communities across the country, one can find a nearly endless assortment of youth programs, each driven by a different combination of participants, philosophy, program design, and structure. Programs are highly variable and even unpredictable in many ways. Even our reflective practitioners were surprised when The Underground, a youth-directed program for seemingly disengaged youth, put out a request for volunteers to teach knitting. Youth-run businesses sell cookies off the cookie cart, screen T-shirts, run thrift stores, manage concession stands, manufacture products for sale, and do hundreds of other interesting things. There is no single or right formula for success, but in general, all can benefit from a periodic "intentionality tune-up." Consider that any program will be stronger if scrutinized regularly under the lens of the framework for developmentally intentional programs. Individuals and organizations can use this framework to raise a variety of important questions that give direction, clarity, and accountability to youth development work in the nonschool hours.

As a reader, ask yourself how you might apply the framework of developmentally intentional programs to advance your own work.

Scan for program strengths

Where am I most intentional in my work, and where am I finding my greatest success? Do these align with my stated program outcomes? Why do I do the work I do? What passions drive me? How can I best make a positive difference? How are the answers to these questions of philosophy reflected in the prevailing ethos of my program?

Make adjustments and course corrections

What do I intentionally do to assure that my activities balance youth-driven ideas and choices with adult-driven guidance and direction? How do I choose program content? Why is it what it is? How do I intentionally vary my methods for learning to accommodate

NEW DIRECTIONS FOR YOUTH DEVELOPMENT • DOI: 10.1002/yd

the strengths and preferences of different learners? How do I intentionally promote physical and psychological safety in my program space? When considering content, methods, and environment, how can I do a more intentional job of being developmentally appropriate, flexible, adventurous, and connected to the world where young people live everyday?

Encourage participant program review

Could I ask colleagues, youth, and parents to review my program according to the model and make suggestions for ways to strengthen these areas? How could I get feedback on how responsive my program is to the cultural and community context of the participants? What could I do to strengthen the program-community connection? How do I involve young people and their families in important aspects of my work? Does my space visibly speak to my community connection? Intentional responsiveness to community and cultural context takes many forms, but it is central to engagement and good fit for participants.

Identify personal and professional strengths of staff

How can I use the model as a tool for professional development? How can I identify the strengths my colleagues and I bring to our work and the areas where I can benefit from further training or mentoring? If I do not live in the community where I work, I may need an intentional plan to connect myself more effectively to the community. If iPod technology and digital music production are passions for the youth but foreign subjects to me, an intentional plan to catch up on new content areas and resources may be in order.

Adapt as a framework for evaluation

If youth relationships with caring adults are a priority, what am I doing to intentionally promote these relationships? How can I be accountable for successes? How can I evaluate this program priority? Can I do more or be more effective, given the young people I work with? How can I measure that? What strategies have I put in place to stimulate nurturing, respectful, caring relationships at all levels? How well are they working? How can I improve the youth-youth relationships in my program? What do I do to stimulate every adult in the program to see the potential in young people and treat them with respect?

In a developmentally intentional program, all the components are deliberately considered and intentionally designed to take the best possible advantage of the positive ethos, young people in their world, and the learning experience based on positive relationships, sensitivity to context, and stimulating activities. All activities benefit from scrutiny to the content, the pedagogy, and the environment at the point of contact with young people.

Youth workers will develop their own questions, the ones that matter to them and inform their work. Programs may look different from place to place, but they are built on the common elements of the model explored here. And all programs can benefit from an intentionality tune-up that makes increasingly explicit the energies that drive these powerful learning programs that take place after school and in extended out-of-school time.

Notes

1. Eccles, J. S., & Gootman, J. A. (eds.). (2002). *Community programs to promote youth development: Committee on community-level programs for youth*. Washington, DC: National Academy Press.

2. Belle, D. (1999). *The after-school lives of children: Alone and with others while parents work*. Mahwah, NJ: Erlbaum.

3. Walker, K., & Larson, R. (2006). Adult-driven youth programs: An oxymoron? *Prevention Researcher, 13*(1), 17–20.

4. Hirsch, B. (2005). *A place to call home: After-school programs for urban youth*. Washington, DC, and New York: American Psychological Association and Teachers College Press.

5. Walker, J., Marczak, M., Blyth, D., & Borden, L. (2005). Designing intentional youth programs: Toward a theory of developmental intentionality. In J. Mahoney, R. Larson, & J. Eccles (Eds.), *Organized activities as contexts of development: Extracurricular activities, after-school and community programs*. Mahwah, NJ: Erlbaum.

6. Bronfenbrenner, U. (1994). Ecological model of human development. In T. Husten & T. N. Postlethwaite (Eds.), *International encyclopedia of education* (Vol. 2, pp. 3–27). Oxford, England: Pergamon Press.

7. Konopka, G. (1973). Requirements for healthy development of adolescent youth. *Adolescence, 8*(31), 2–25; Resnick, M. D. (2000). Protective factors,

resiliency, and healthy youth development. *Adolescent Medicine: State of the Art Reviews, 11*(1), 157–164.

8. McLaughlin, M. (2000). *Community counts: How youth organizations matter for youth development.* Washington, DC: Public Education Network.

9. Catalano, R. F., Berglund, M. L., Ryan, J. A., Lonczak, H. S., & Hawkins, J. D. (1999). *Positive youth development in the United States: Research findings on evaluations of positive youth development programs.* Seattle: University of Washington School of Social Work; Quinn, J. (2001, Spring). Harvard Family Research Project: A conversation with Jane Quinn. *Evaluation Exchange, 7*(2), 8–9.

10. Larson, R., & Walker, K. (2006, May). Learning about the "real world" in an urban arts youth program. *Journal of Adolescent Research, 21*(3), 244–268.

11. Bigelow, M. (2006, April 11). *The social and cultural capital a Somali refugee teen brings to school.* Paper presented at the American Educational Research Association, San Francisco.

12. The names of this program and the ones that follow have been changed because the brief descriptions here do not represent the full scope of the actual programs in the Minneapolis–St. Paul metropolitan area.

13. Calhoun, D., & Saito, R. (2005). *The Howland road trip: A journey from research to practice.* Keynote address themes for Howland Symposium on DVD format, University of Minnesota, Minneapolis.

14. Special thanks to the reflective practitioners Rebecca Saito, Delroy Calhoun, and Christine Ganzlin for their stories and insights into intentional strategies to reach youth in the middle years.

15. The Howland Family Endowment for Youth Leadership Development is supported by the Minnesota 4-H Foundation. Recognized experts in research, policy, and practice serve as endowed chair for a year and contribute their expertise to the advancement of work in the field.

16. Milbrey McLaughlin made this apt observation at the Howland Symposium at the University of Minnesota in 2002.

17. Tyler, R. W. (1949). *Basic principles of curriculum and instruction.* Chicago: University of Chicago Press.

JOYCE A. WALKER *is a professor and community youth development educator at the Center for 4-H and Community Youth Development at the University of Minnesota where she also gives leadership to the Youth Development Leadership M.Ed. Program in the College of Education and Human Development.*

Quality in youth programs happens at the point of service and is driven by staff intentionality, supportive professional communities, and aligned system priorities.

6

Improving quality at the point of service

Charles Smith, Tom Akiva, Dominique Arrieux, Monica M. Jones

THE JOURNEY INTO MIDDLE CHILDHOOD frequently involves a journey into the community of an after-school program, weekend club, or summer camp. Although out-of-school-time settings are less formal than school in academic requirements, they have the potential to provide key developmental experiences: relationship building, learning, and self- and social exploration. In this chapter, we draw on a decade of experience from staff at the High/Scope Foundation to develop and validate training models, assessment tools, and improvement methods for use in youth program settings. Through this work, we have become convinced that although highly committed and intentional staff drive youth access to high-quality programming, reliance on individual staff is not enough. Regulatory systems and professional communities must also get focused on quality at the point of service.

We outline a model for youth program quality: what it is, where it occurs, and how it can be effectively and consistently produced.

NEW DIRECTIONS FOR YOUTH DEVELOPMENT, NO. 112, WINTER 2006 © WILEY PERIODICALS, INC.
Published online in Wiley InterScience (www.interscience.wiley.com) • DOI: 10.1002/yd.195

We argue, as shown in Figure 6.1, that *quality* is best defined as access to key developmental experiences and that this occurs at the point of service: the place where youth and program intersect. The point of service is embedded within two additional levels: professional community and system. When these levels also focus on quality at the point of service, a culture of intentionality and accountability for quality can emerge that sets priorities, communicates values, and supports action on the part of the frontline staff.

Frontline intentionality

Walker and colleagues provide a theory of "developmental intentionality" that nicely defines the priorities and values that support optimal program experience for early adolescents (also see the previous chapter in this volume). Being intentional about quality requires that attention to long-term developmental outcomes permeates the program; that young people need to be active collaborators in selecting strategies and defining the specific learning opportunities; and finally, that there must be a good fit between

Figure 6.1. Point of service and key developmental experiences

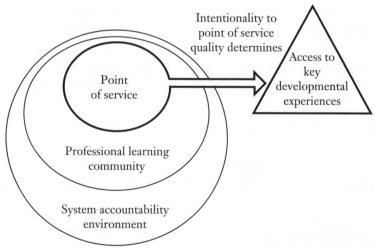

young people and the learning opportunities that they take part in.[1] But what does it take to actually develop and deliver this high level of professional understanding and craft knowledge?

Minimally, meeting this definition of intentionality about quality might mean that staff must plan how they use time, understand how the roles of staff and youth may blend together, and flex the content and purpose of the program to fit youth interests and needs. They also need to figure out how to get enough time in the day to find or coordinate the human and material resources necessary to bring these actions into existence. Our experience suggests that even when individual staff can achieve these heroic levels of effort, they are difficult to maintain for long unless other staff, administrators, funders, and regulators are all focused intentionally on quality at the point of service.

It is important to note that "intentional" is not the same as "structured." As Barton Hirsch points out in his recent book about urban after-school programs, one must not discount the importance of informal opportunities to have fun and to "just be kids in neighborhoods where this is otherwise impossible."[2] It is not structure but intentionality—a deliberate focus on creating opportunities for youth to have key developmental experiences—that makes the difference.

Metrics of quality

Today several powerful models of positive youth development,[3] research on features of program settings,[4] and community-based systems of supports and opportunities[5] represent a rough consensus about what quality programming looks like for kids between nine and fifteen years old. Further, several methods of practice have been developed that provide guidance about the relative importance of specific supports and opportunities and how to knit the elements together in a way that feels coherent to both staff and youth.[6] However, the field lacks metrics—descriptive standards and aligned assessments—that allow organizations and individual staff to know how well they are implementing these best practices.

The development of quality metrics has been challenging because the defining features of quality for early adolescents are human interactions and forms of authentic pedagogy[7] that are not easily counted. These features are best described as frontline staff performances and are fundamentally different in nature and frequency from more physical elements of quality. For example, well-defined interest areas (a hallmark of quality for preschool children) or an emergency plan (near-universal licensing requirement), once in the building, consistently delivers its effect, and both are easily counted. However, providing youth with a successful experience of project planning requires a staff member to have a fairly complex skill set, and it is more likely to work if at least some of the youth have practiced the skills before. Further, staff performances to establish a sense of belonging in a program—welcoming, using positive body language, and active listening—may need to be redelivered hourly, daily, or weekly to have an effect.

When quality standards that are appropriate for early adolescents are in place, observational assessment is a critical source of verification that what staff think is happening is actually happening. Because we use words to describe quality practices, the meaning of quality flows through language that describes our beliefs and goals and that is based on referents that are rooted in experience that can diverge widely across individuals.[8] It is entirely possible for a youth worker or teacher to agree that quality is critical, to interpret his or her own performance as meeting high standards of quality, and to be incorrect.

In our recent work, two tools have helped to grow staff intentionality about quality: a multidimensional rubric for point-of-service quality and the aligned technology of observational assessment.

Point-of-service quality

Focusing at the point of service frames quality in terms of a youth perspective because their access to key experiences (although not necessarily their perceptions) defines quality. It also raises a key equity issue: Are key experiences available to all of the youth who attend? Point-of-service quality is particularly relevant to programs serving early adolescents because the *point* (purpose) of the program—rooted as it is in patterns of human interaction—occurs at the *point* (place and time) where youth and staff meet.

The elements of point-of-service quality are depicted in Figure 6.2. Although the pyramid is the product of extensive field research, the ideas that it contains are not new. The bottom two levels define safety and support in a youth-serving program. The safety level contains many of the material items and fixed processes found in licensing regulations whereas the supportive-environment level lists the necessary human and material supports for participatory learning

Figure 6.2. The pyramid of program quality

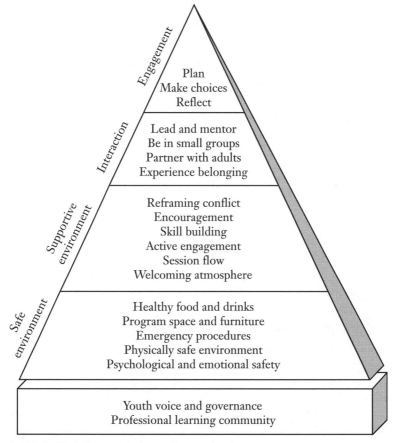

© 2005 by High/Scope Foundation. Reprinted with permission.

and a sense of belonging. The interaction level describes collaborative behaviors that follow from effective group collaboration and productivity. The top level, engagement, taps higher-order processes that build motivation, buy-in, and individuation into program processes. The vertical organization of the pyramid implies that some elements of quality are foundational and must exist before others. In parallel with Abraham Maslow's hierarchy of needs,[9] the pyramid suggests that safety is a prerequisite to higher-order social and cognitive operations.

Youth program quality assessment

Each level of the pyramid also represents a validated multi-item subscale in the Youth Program Quality Assessment (PQA), an observational quality assessment tool developed for use in out-of-school-time settings.[10] The indicators, items, and subscales of the Youth PQA are metrics to describe key developmental experiences, and the instrument measures both the presence of and all youths' access to those experiences.

Efforts to validate the Youth PQA have provided opportunities to use data from more than five hundred quality observations to test the theory of quality that the pyramid represents and to describe the state of quality in the field in these terms. Findings across several samples include the following:[11]

- Point-of-service quality is organized in a hierarchical structure: scores are highest for Safe Environment, decrease as you go up the pyramid, and are lowest in the subscales of Interaction and Engagement.
- Point-of-service quality is rooted in the performances of individual staff: scores vary substantially around the performances of individual staff within organizations, meaning that at least some low-quality performances are present in most organizations.
- Point-of-service quality is not strongly related to content: scores were not associated with the content of an offering or an explicit purpose, academic or enrichment.

• Higher-order experiences were more strongly related to motivation-related outcomes: scores from the top two subscales were most strongly associated with youth reports of interest, sense of growth, and skill building.

An important feature is that scores tend to be lowest in exactly the areas most likely to add value for early adolescent participants—experiences related to purposeful interactions and sustained engagement—and the kinds of experiences most likely to require developmental intentionality on the part of staff to create.

Quality in multilevel systems

Quality is defined as access to key developmental experiences, and those experiences occur for youth at the point of service. However, factors outside the program space strongly regulate quality, as suggested in Figure 6.1, and our experience suggests that policymakers, funders, and program administrators lack tools to communicate priorities and core values about point-of-service quality, even if they want to do so. Under these conditions, unsupported or underskilled frontline staff tend to revert to the easiest models: the "large-group, high-discipline, content-focused" school-day approach or the laissez faire "keep the kids safe and let them play" child-care model. Both lack fit with the developmental needs of early adolescents[12] and are likely to attract only kids whose parents make them come.

Professional learning community

The professional learning community is created in formal staff meetings, in less formal hallway conversations, and across programs when staff attend system-level meetings or conferences. The model of a professional community that is effectively focused on quality at the point of service is similar to that which Walker and colleagues call "an ethos of positive youth development": the idea that all staff are involved in a general spirit and way of working that embraces positive youth development.

However, the literature on professional learning communities in schools provides several important lessons about getting the professional learning community focused on point-of-service quality. First, in schools where academic achievement is the goal, it is possible to get the same poor results from either disorganized groups of staff (ineffective professional learning community) or effectively organized communities of staff who are not focused on academic achievement; either way, academic achievement is not likely to rise due to intentional actions on the part of staff.[13] Second, we know that the dominant pattern of professional development (in-service training) is not rooted in the selection of naturally occurring teams, follow-up support for implementation, or staff consultation about application to the instructional context.[14] The point here is the same in both cases: program leaders must steer the professional community toward a set of shared priorities and values that actually change the performances of staff and youth.

We argue that one of the best ways to get professional communities intentionally focused on the point of service is the use of quality metrics. However, our recent efforts to survey staff in the after-school field suggest that these tools are either not available or not functional for most direct staff and their supervisors. In a recent survey,[15] over four hundred direct staff in after-school programs reported how frequently they use data of any sort (youth preference surveys, quality assessment, child outcomes measures, evaluation results from larger studies) for purposes of program planning. In samples from two states, less than 10 percent of direct staff and less than 40 percent of site supervisors reported that they had ever used data for program planning or improvement. Of those who had used data to support planning, comments like the following were common: "The discussed policies/procedures were never implemented. We just attended the meetings—no real say in anything." Further, when asked if they were aware of existing quality standards (they did in fact exist) for their programs, less than 3 percent of program staff and less than 25 percent of site supervisors had ever seen the standards.

Systems accountability environment

The outer ring in Figure 6.1 depicts the systems accountability environment and is considered the accountability setting in which a youth program exists. Individuals in the systems accountability environment may include funders, government, and youth program intermediaries. By building accountability requirements and communicating that quality is a priority (adoption of quality assessment or standards), these key players provide a platform for staff intentionality about quality.

Unfortunately, existing structures of regulation—accountability, accreditation, licensing, state standards—frequently hold staff and youth accountable for rules of operation and coverage of content rather than the efficacy of their performances. When concerned with point-of-service quality, these metrics tend to focus on the bottom of the pyramid. In Youth PQA-to-standards alignments with eight national, state, county, and city-level sets of out-of-school-time program standards,[16] alignments conducted by High/Scope and external groups[17] concluded that existing standards did not provide depth in the critical areas of Interaction and Engagement. This suggests that the regulatory environment does not prioritize quality at the point of service and does not reinforce the kind of developmental intentionality that defines optimal programming for early adolescents.

Cultures of intentionality

How can accountability policies support intentionality about point-of-service quality in programs that serve early adolescents? Further, how can accountability create cultures of intentionality about point-of-service quality that are reinforced across levels of organization? The term accountability is used here to refer to administrative priorities that have staff performance as their object. Current accountability structures in the field—standards and quality assessment—do not effectively prioritize or validate point-of-service quality and, therefore, cannot empower staff to act with the skilled, artful intentionality that it takes to cocreate and sustain key experiences on a daily basis. When

NEW DIRECTIONS FOR YOUTH DEVELOPMENT • DOI: 10.1002/yd

decision makers, administrators, and supervisors prioritize point-of-service quality, the efforts of direct staff will yield greater effect.

The model depicted in Figure 6.3 was developed through work over the past two years with nearly a dozen out-of-school-time systems and a handful of individual programs. This process begins at the systems accountability environment by working with decision makers to secure buy-in to the importance of point-of-service quality and use of observational assessment. Next, the model moves to the professional learning community and uses quality data and various data-driven improvement techniques to support program leaders as they get their staff focused on making positive incremental change in quality ratings. Finally, and only after these earlier steps, the model directly addresses the performance of frontline staff through traditional training. This sequence flips the currently entrenched improvement approach—get frontline staff trained and hope for the best—upside down. Every step of the process, however, is designed to help participants at all levels focus on the point of

Figure 6.3. Program quality improvement process

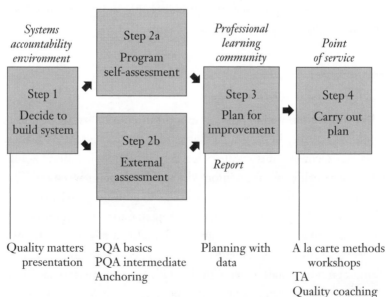

service, with observational quality assessment as the lens of best practice.

Anecdotal evidence suggests that when a network or community successfully makes it to step 4 of the process (in Figure 6.3), frontline staff tend to be primed for improvement. Accumulating anecdotal evidence from our work suggests that short doses of training then have a strong or stronger impact than longer doses without the multilevel process.[18]

Case examples from the field

In the past few years, we have gained substantial anecdotal feedback from individuals at all three levels: frontline staff, program supervisors, and system decision makers. The following case examples demonstrate how the concepts explored in this article play out in real life.

Example 1: Building a system of accountability

In this case, great effort was made by individuals at the network level to build an effective after-school system of accountability. Point-of-service quality was made a priority, and efforts were made to assess the quality of after-school environments in a way that engaged and empowered staff. The county created a set of quality standards that reflected top-of-the-pyramid values, adopted a quality assessment tool (a customized version of the Youth PQA), provided training on the assessment tool for all site supervisors and some additional staff, required all sites to conduct a self-assessment, and conducted external assessment at baseline in each program.

The narrative that follows was provided by a staff member at Prime Time, Inc., Palm Beach County, the countywide organization that facilitated the quality improvement project:

Over the past sixteen months, Quality Advisors at Prime Time engaged staff from several youth programs in a series of steps that allowed for looking at the overall picture of program quality using the Palm Beach County Program Quality Assessment tool (PBC-PQA). The steps included obtaining a baseline assessment, participating in a self-assessment process, developing a plan for improvement based on assessments and receiving coaching support through Prime Time.

Quality advisors from Prime Time supported program directors in training program staff on obtaining anecdotal evidence about what was taking place in their programs. Staff was scheduled to observe each other and then enter into a dialogue about quality in their program. At the end of the self-assessment process, many directors were surprised. "I was completely shocked," stated one program director, "to see that my staff remained objective. They pointed out the areas where we fell short, especially when it came to working together with youth, communicating with them, and getting their input about the program. I do see now that my staff and I need some training on what it really means to engage youth." Another director commented that his staff took the work very seriously, and they began to take note of the way they spoke to one another and the youth in the program. They started to reflect on not so much what they did with youth but how they did things. "It seems that we have become a little more conscious of what we say and how we say it."

For program staff, use of the PBC-PQA introduced a common language for youth development work. As one director pointed out, "When I first attended training, it was just information for me about good youth practice. But when I actually picked up the tool and worked with my staff on observing one another and what we do with our kids, that's when it all made sense. I am ready to take the training again because now I understand the terminology and can relate it back to what I have seen." Many program directors began to request specific training based on the improvement goals they set in response to quality data. We started to hear more talk about giving youth opportunities to reflect (Figure 6.2, level 4), effective ways to engage youth in small group activities (Figure 6.2, level 3), creating a sense of belonging in a program (Figure 6.2, level 3), establishing and implementing youth advisory councils (Figure 6.2, base level), and engaging youth in discussions and conversations that are safe, honest, and open.

Example 2: Building a quality program

As a second case example, the director of a large all-volunteer after-school program in Detroit (REACH Youth Programs, Inc.) describes how she used the concept of point-of-service quality and the Youth PQA to improve experiences for early adolescents. The program director was part of a neighborhood-level intervention to raise quality funded by the Skillman Foundation in Detroit that again provided clear communication about point-of-service quality as a priority.[19] Through the initiative, this staff member received substantial methods and assessment training focused on point-of-service quality, and the funder adopted the Youth PQA as a mandatory quality metric for programs in the project.

Each day at the after-school program, we had a couple of hours set aside for homework help. The middle school students got out earlier than the elementary school students, so they would spend that time doing their homework and socializing. Before long, all of them were either finished or without homework and began playing around with their peers. Naturally, this became a distraction to those who still had homework to finish as well as to the elementary school students who were arriving to begin their homework time.

In an effort to increase the quality of youth-service delivery, my remedy for this was to engage the middle school students by having them act as tutors and mentors to the elementary school students. I would place one or two middle school students at each table with four or five elementary school students. This promoted a sense of belonging for the students (Figure 6.2, level 3) in that they were given the opportunity to work in small groups (Figure 6.2, level 3). It also made the relationships among the students more inclusive because before students usually only interacted with students within their own age group. Adult program staff would circulate and provide support as needed (Figure 6.2, level 3), but for the most part, the middle school students had it under control. This gave them a genuine opportunity to practice leadership skills (Figure 6.2, level 3).

Before implementing this plan of action, middle school students would exhibit negative behaviors, some conflict, or just leave after their homework time was over. Engaging them in facilitation, such as leading songs during snack time or helping to teach an offering such as dance or basketball gave them a reason to stick around. As a result, students began to identify more strongly with the program, and a decrease in negative behavior and conflict followed (Figure 6.2, level 2).

Conclusion

It is a good time in history for programs that serve youth during the nonschool hours. Public attention and resources are beginning to recognize the impact that these hours have on youth, and many exceptional programs are making measurable contributions to positive change in the lives of youth. The challenge before the field now is how to make high quality the norm. In this chapter, we argue that the best way to do this is to get the system, the supervisors, and the frontline staff focused on quality at the point of service. The youth development field must move past the current regulatory consensus that holds programs accountable for safety and content—and little more. Further, current resources dedicated to training, accountability, and evaluation might be more efficiently and effectively used to support these ultimate developmental and learning purposes. Quality metrics can support staff to be more intentional about strengths they already have. By creating cultures of accountability for quality that cross levels of organization, site priorities, program values, and staff performance can be aligned to produce optimal developmental and learning experiences for the youth of middle childhood.

Notes

1. Walker, J., Marczak, M., Blyth, D., & Borden, L. (2005). Designing youth development programs: Toward a theory of developmental intentionality. In J. L. Mahoney, R. W. Larson, & J. S. Eccles (Eds.), *Organized activities as contexts of development: Extracurricular activities, after-school and community programs* (pp. 399–418). Mahwah, NJ: Erlbaum.

2. Hirsch, B. J. (2005). *A place to call home: After-school programs for urban youth.* New York: Teachers College Press, p. 171.

3. Larson, R. (2000). Toward a psychology of positive youth development. *American Psychologist, 55*(1), 170–183.

4. Eccles, J., & Gootman, J. A. (Eds.). (2002). *Community programs to promote youth development. Committee on community-level programs for youth.* Washington, DC: National Academy Press.

5. Gambone, M. A., Klem, A. M., & Connel, J. P. (2002). *Finding out what matters for youth: Testing key links in a community action framework for youth development.* Philadelphia: Youth Development Strategies and Institute for Research and Reform in Education.

6. Several youth work approaches have been developed that organize knowledge and methodology from the perspective of the youth worker, with more or less focus on point of service: Advancing Youth Development (http://www.nti.aed.org), Bringing Yourself to Work (http://www.wcwonline.org/bringselftowork/index.htm), High/Scope Youth Work Methods (http://www.highscope.org/EducationalPrograms/Adolescent/homepage.html), and the Search Institute 40 Developmental Assets (http://www.searchinstitute.org).

7. The term is included here to point out that academic instruction during the after-school hours can be held to similar standards of quality accountabil-

ity. Newman, F. M., Marks, H. M., & Gamoran, A. (1995). *Authentic pedagogy: Standards that boost student performance.* Madison, WI: Center for the Organization and Restructuring of Schools.

8. Pianta, R. (2003). *Standardized classroom observations from pre-K to third grade: A mechanism for improving quality classroom experiences during the P-3 years.* Unpublished manuscript; Hilberg, R. S., Waxman, H. C., & Tharp, R. G. (2003). Introduction: Purposes and perspectives on classroom observation research. In H. C. Waxman, R. G. Tharp, & R. S. Hilberg (Eds.), *Observational research in U.S. classrooms.* Cambridge: Cambridge University Press.

9. Maslow, A. H. (1943). A theory of human motivation. *Psychological Review, 50,* 370–396.

10. High/Scope Educational Research Foundation. (2005). *Youth program quality assessment: Administration manual.* Ypsilanti, MI: High/Scope Press. Several other high-quality tools have been introduced in the past few years. See the forthcoming report from the Forum for Youth Investment, which describes several new quality assessment tools, including the Youth PQA, that have undergone rigorous validation studies (http://www.forumforyouthinvestment.org).

11. Smith, C. (2004). *Youth Program Quality Assessment validation study: Wave-1 findings for reliability and validity analyses.* Report to the W. T. Grant Foundation; Smith, C. (2005a). *The Youth Program Quality Assessment validation study: Findings for instrument validation.* Report available from the High/Scope Foundation at http://www.highscope.org/EducationalPrograms/Adolescent/homepage.htm; Smith, C. (2005b). *Measuring quality in Michigan's 21st Century afterschool programs: The Youth PQA self-assessment pilot study.* Report available from the High/Scope Foundation at http://www.highscope.org/EducationalPrograms/Adolescent/homepage.htm; Smith, C. (2005c, December 19). *What matters for after-school quality?* Presentation to the W. T. Grant Foundation After-school Grantees Meeting.

12. Eccles, J. S., & Midgley, C. (1989). Stage-environment fit: Developmentally appropriate classrooms for young adolescents. In C. Ames & R. Ames (Eds.), *Research on motivation in education,* Vol. 3, *Goals and cognitions.* Orlando, FL: Academic Press; Erickson, E. H. (1968). *Identity: Youth and crisis.* New York: Norton.

13. Bryk, A. S., Camburn, E., & Seashore-Louis, K. (1999). Professional community in Chicago elementary schools: Facilitating factors and organizational consequences. *Educational Administration Quarterly, 35,* 751–781; Halverson, R., Grigg, J., Prichett, R., & Thomas, C. (2005). *The new instructional leadership: Creating data-driven instructional systems in schools.* Madison: Wisconsin Center for Education Research, University of Wisconsin-Madison.

14. Desmione, L. M., Porter, A. C., Garet, M. S., Yoon, K. S., & Birman, B. F. (2002). Effects of professional development on teachers' instruction: Results from a three-year longitudinal study. *Educational Evaluation and Policy Analysis, 24*(2), 81–112.

15. Smith, C., Akiva, T., & Henry, B. (2006, March). *Quality in the out–of-school-time sector: Insights from the Youth Program Quality Assessment Validation Study.* Paper presented at the biannual meeting of the Society for Research in Adolescence, San Francisco.

16. National After-School Association Accreditation Standards (http://www. naaweb.org/accreditation/htm); Palm Beach County Standards for After-School Quality (http://primetimepbc.org/p&i_initiatives.asp); Youth, Sports and Recreation Commission for the City of Detroit (http://www.ysrc.org/); The After-School Corporation of New York quality assessment standards (http://www.tascorp.org/programs/building).

17. *Report to the Youth, Sports and Recreation Commission of the City of Detroit conducted by the Center for Urban Studies at Wayne State University* (2005).

18. With funding from the W. T. Grant Foundation, High/Scope is currently undertaking a randomized field trial of the Youth Program Quality Intervention in one hundred sites to test this hypothesis.

19. Smith, C. (2004, August). *Lasting solutions: A vision for positive youth development across the Nolan State Fair area.* Final report to the Skillman Foundation, Detroit.

CHARLES SMITH *manages youth-level research, consulting, and direct service at the High/Scope Educational Research Foundation. His interests include policy, research on learning environments, and civic literacy.*

TOM AKIVA, *senior specialist at the High/Scope Foundation, is the lead developer of youth-level training content and online services. Previously he worked as a middle school teacher and camp director.*

DOMINIQUE ARRIEUX *manages after-school improvement programs for Prime Time, Inc., of Palm Beach County. She has more than fifteen years of experience implementing and promoting nontraditional education programs in the nonprofit sector.*

MONICA M. JONES, *a specialist at the High/Scope Foundation, conducts training and consulting related to quality improvement. Previously she coordinated the REACH after-school program in Detroit.*

Youth workers encounter numerous dilemmas in their daily practice, including tension created by relating to youth in a professional versus a personal way.

7

Dilemmas of youth work: Balancing the professional and personal

Kathrin C. Walker, Reed W. Larson

BEING EFFECTIVE AND INTENTIONAL as a youth practitioner involves not just planning. It includes being able to react intelligently to the difficult situations that arise. Across forms of practice from health care settings to social service, practitioners regularly confront complex dilemmas that emerge in their daily work. They face situations where competing objectives, values, and warrants come into conflict.[1] For youth practitioners, these situations can pit the developmental needs of youth, ethical concerns, administrative requirements, and other considerations against each other. The quality of a youth development program depends significantly on how staff respond to these challenging situations.

One frequent class of daily dilemma puts youth workers' professional versus their personal relationship with youth into tension. On the one hand, they have a responsibility to relate to youth within professional standards, from a position of authority. They need to ensure youths' personal safety, represent the interests of the organization, encourage or lead activities that foster youths'

This research was supported by grants from the William T. Grant Foundation. For more about our research, go to http://web.aces.uiuc.edu/youthdev.

development, and draw on their knowledge and stature as someone who is older and wiser. This may require enforcing rules, exercising leadership, and keeping an eye on implications of program activities that youth may not be thinking about. At some level, they need to maintain a position as an adult.

On the other hand, youth workers are often effective in their jobs by relating to youth in more personal, informal, and peerlike ways. Leaders find this more personal bond helpful in building rapport, motivating youth, and gaining their trust. To cultivate personal relationships, they may share feelings and develop caring and authentic friendships with youth. It is argued that youth development settings play uniquely valuable roles in teens' lives because they bridge the world of youth and the "real world" they must enter as adults[2] and that youth workers are effective because they straddle these two worlds.[3] Their ability to understand and participate in youths' world may allow them to provide guidance and direction that parents, teachers, and other adults are not trusted to give.

But there are underlying tensions between relating to youth in a professional versus a personal way. The demands of being a professional and an authority can come into conflict with those of being a sympathetic participant. In the words of one program leader, "That's a really tough thing to learn and to figure out: how to really be a friend to young people, how to meet them where they're at. But the challenge is to take them where they haven't been." These tensions can become acute in specific situations in daily youth practice. For example, this same leader was torn about whether to dismiss a sympathetic but troubled girl in their six-week summer employment program when, despite his numerous attempts to be empathic and reason with her, she repeatedly disrupted program activities. Youth workers find themselves in daily dilemmas that put their professional and personal relationships with youth in conflict with each other.

In this chapter, we describe our research on these dilemmas, and then we present two examples of dilemmas that deal specifically with the tension between relating to youth in a professional versus a personal way.

Analysis of daily dilemmas

In our research, we are trying to understand the types of dilemmas that adult leaders of youth programs encounter in their daily work with young people. The dilemmas come from an in-depth longitudinal study of ongoing experiences in twelve high-quality urban and rural programs for high school-aged youth. Transcripts from 125 interviews with the adult program leaders, 788 interviews with youth, and 167 site observations by our staff were used to identify specific challenging situations that these leaders encountered.

Our analysis found that leaders encountered difficult situations frequently. We have created a database that contains the 250 dilemmas that we identified as well as information on how the leaders responded to each and the outcomes of the leaders' responses on program activities and the youth. We are employing matrix-based qualitative analyses techniques[4] to understand and categorize the dilemmas, analyze the leaders' responses, and evaluate the outcomes. Although these programs dealt with youth somewhat older than the middle years that are the focus of this volume, there are underlying similarities in the types of dilemmas that would be found in programs for younger youth.

Our analysis of these dilemmas indicates that a sizable number involved a primary tension between the demands of relating to youth in a professional versus a personal way. Here are a few short examples of situations that created this type of tension:

- A youth invites the adult leader to a party at her home.
- A fourteen-year-old girl confides to her adult leader that she is concerned she might be pregnant. The girl does not have the money for a home pregnancy test and does not appear likely to trust her predicament with anyone else.
- Two youth members become involved in a romantic relationship, and both seek personal advice about the relationship from the adult leader.

These situations are complex. They involve dealing with multiple considerations. They may pit moral, developmental, motivational, institutional, and other concerns against each other. Do you attend the party to understand and participate in the youth's world, or do you decline to avoid becoming too intimate with the youth? Does one help the girl get the pregnancy test, knowing she is unlikely to turn to anyone else, or do you try to get her to appropriate professionals despite her adamant opposition? Do you provide judicious guidance as a trusted friend to both partners in the romantic relationship, or do you try to set a professional boundary to avoid being perceived as allying yourself with one or the other?

It is important to better understand the complexity of these types of professional versus personal dilemmas and to learn how effective youth workers respond to them. Let us look at two further examples in depth. For each, we describe the dilemma, the leader's response, and the outcome for the youth's developmental experience.

When to share personal information with youth

The first example concerns when should youth practitioners share information about themselves with youth? "Linda"[5] was the facilitator of Girl Power, an all-female youth group that holds weekly sessions on issues determined by the youth, often issues of identity. Over several years, Linda worked hard to create a space where the girls felt comfortable sharing their experiences and opinions. The dilemma was that as part of their discussions, the girls often asked Linda about her personal life. For example, when the group toured a local women's health clinic, some of the girls asked Linda whether she had had premarital sex. In a discussion about the upcoming prom, the girls inquired how Linda had dealt with pressure to have sex on her prom night. In another session on fathers, the topic of corporal punishment arose, and a girl asked Linda how she will discipline her newborn son.

In these situations, Linda had to decide when to share her personal life stories with the girls. On the one hand, she wanted to build rapport and trust with the youth and to model and create a

NEW DIRECTIONS FOR YOUTH DEVELOPMENT • DOI: 10.1002/yd

space where they felt comfortable sharing personal information. On the other hand, Linda had a professional obligation to set appropriate boundaries on what she shared.

Leader's response

In response to this repeated dilemma, Linda had developed internal rules to guide her decision making. First, she would ask herself whether divulging a personal experience had a teaching purpose or was an opportunity for her to model something that would be useful to the youth. So, for example, in a discussion on anger management, she shared how in arguments with her husband she can be passive-aggressive and not really say what she feels. She explained, "I feel like that's an appropriate way to share because you have to model as an adult that you, too, struggle with things." Linda saw that by opening up, by relating to them personally, she could model to the youth. It would provide them with an example of an adult struggling with issues that were not that distinct from issues in the youth's lives. It also would help the youth open up and make them more comfortable with her.

Professionally, Linda had developed a sense of what she saw to be appropriate boundaries. She described how some adults divulge to youth for shock value or to prove, "Well, I've had experiences, or I've done this or that." Linda felt that these were not appropriate reasons to share something, and she set an internal rule not to divulge in these ways. So in the case of corporal punishment, Linda shared her opinion and her own personal history of abuse, but she did so in a way that did not "drop a bomb on these young people" and assumed they could handle it. Linda said, "You need to talk to them as though they are teenagers."

Outcomes

Linda acknowledged that navigating this dilemma is something with which she continually grappled. She tried to make decisions about disclosure of personal information on a case-by-case basis, carefully attending to the balance between revealing when there is a teaching purpose and censoring herself when it is in the best interest of the youth's development to do so. Our interviews with the youth suggested that these guidelines seemed to work well. They reported that they valued hearing Linda's stories and learning from them and appreciated her openness and honesty. Youth stated that the group feels like a safe place to discuss any issues that were going on in their lives, in part because of Linda's willingness to self-disclose. They also reported respecting her and appreciated that the program was for and about them.

It is interesting to note that midway through our study, a new facilitator joined this tight-knit group. She was not as comfortable revealing personal information about herself to the girls. In interviews with the youth, they indicated that although they accepted the new leader's decision to not answer their questions, they did not feel as close and felt she was too distant and motherly.

How to deal with a problematic choreographer

The second example involved tension between the personal and the professional on a much larger stage: a dance program in which over one hundred youth were preparing for an upcoming show. Beth was a highly experienced artistic director whose approach to youth development involved cultivating personal connections to youth as individuals and as a large group. She encouraged them to express their feelings on and off stage; she would come early and stay late to talk with individuals about personal issues; and she frequently expressed her own joy and sadness to them in ways that were constructive, like Linda did. She had hired a local, professionally experienced choreographer who turned out, however, to have a different style. He was abrupt, provided little praise, and focused all his attention on dancers with lead roles, which violated Beth's stated philosophy that every student mattered equally. The youth reported being frustrated, stressed, and angered by his approach. A member of the chorus described going home crying one night after he put her down.

Having hired the choreographer, Beth felt a professional obligation to give him a chance. She communicated concerns to him in private but felt she could not confront or contradict him publicly in front of the youth. However, she could see his effect on the students. She felt his approach was undercutting the climate of mutual care and concern she had cultivated, that the sense of confidence youth needed to be creative and grow was being "damaged." Things came to a head for Beth on a night when the choreographer insulted the student assistant choreographer, Jake, and assigned him mundane clerical tasks. This public event had a chilling effect on the entire group, and Jake wanted to walk out.

Leader's response

Beth, however, told Jake, "No, you're gonna sit here by me, and we're gonna work on this music." Then she spent the night working with him and giving support to students. "The whole night, that's what I was doing. I was going around working the crowd. Like, I saw a bunch of them having back massages, so I went over and participated in it or made jokes in another part of the building just to try to keep their spirits up. I was doing some damage control."

After that night, Beth fired the choreographer and provided a discreetly worded explanation about "artistic differences" to the students. Although enumerating the grievances against him would have been an easy way to gain favor with the youth, she felt that would be professionally inappropriate. Beth then appointed Jake, who had substantial prior experience as a dancer and choreographer, to his position. In the subsequent days, she worked hard with the students to reestablish morale, particularly among the dance-line members who had been ignored.

Outcomes

Beth's navigation of this unfolding dilemma shows a skilled and carefully timed balancing of the complex tension youth practitioners can face between the professional and personal. She had followed her professional obligation to give the choreographer a chance and not express her private feelings about him, even though that compromised her personal relationship with the youth. But she also found ways to express empathy, provide support, and maintain her personal relationships with the youth as best she could as the situation permitted. Indeed, a few weeks after the choreographer was fired, the amicable climate on set was restored, and the quality of the students' work improved.

Many of the youth we interviewed understood the dilemma Beth was in and learned from how she navigated this and numerous other challenges over the course of multiple performances. At the end of our study, a number of youth identified Beth as a role model who had influenced them, for example, to go into teaching or the ministry. We think her effectiveness as a role model lay in the strength, grace, and intelligence she displayed in handling these types of difficult situations of practice. She demonstrated to them that it was possible to be a professional, to uphold professional standards, yet relate to the people you work with in a caring, personal way.

Conclusion

Analyzing and understanding these types of dilemmas is important. Our research shows that the daily life of youth practice is replete with these kinds of challenging decision situations. Current efforts to define and encourage program quality often fail to take into account the complexity of practitioners' experience "on the ground" in everyday practice. It is one thing to identify the features of good programs[6] or set quality standards for programs. It is often another matter to understand how to achieve these features or standards when facing the complex dilemmas of real-world practice.

Situations involving tension between the professional and personal are only one category among the many dilemmas identified in our research.[7] But they are instructive. The situations we described for Linda and Beth showed a complexity that cannot be reduced to a simple equation. (Indeed, our accounts simplified the multiple considerations in each case.) These situations required them to act within the demands of multiple professional standards and from their position of authority. At the same time, they had to consider the ways in which being empathic, being a friend, and being a member of the youths' world allowed them to be effective in their jobs.

Both Linda and Beth responded to these situations by trying to apply principles, but their approach was by no means formulaic. Linda had developed rules about when it was beneficial to share her personal experiences and when this sharing could have adverse consequences. Beth felt she had a professional obligation to give assistants she hired a fair chance to do their job. But in the situation we described, she worked hard to reconcile it with her strong commitment to relating to youth in personal and caring ways. Although these practitioners had internal guidelines, they responded to situations on a case-by-case basis that considered the costs and benefits of different choices in a particular situation.

This research has shown us that, although good leaders are not able to find a perfect solution for every difficult situation—sometimes their solutions fail or even make things worse—they are impressively creative and intelligent in responding to difficult situations in ways that address complex competing demands. Further, in many cases they found solutions that seemed to turn the dilemma into an opportunity to facilitate youths' development.

To improve the quality of programs, research, policy, and training needs to give more attention to what happens in the thick of daily practice. The definition of quality needs to include youth workers' practical knowledge and their ability to intentionally read and respond to complex situations like the ones in the case examples in ways that maintain conditions for youth to grow and learn.

Notes

1. Schwandt, T. A. (2003). Back to the rough ground: Beyond theory to practice in evaluation. *Evaluation, 9*(3), 353–364.

2. Noam, G. G., & Tillinger, J. R. (2004). After-school as intermediary space: Theory and typology of partnerships. In G. G. Noam (ed.), *After-school worlds: Creating space for development and learning* (pp. 75–113). New Directions for Youth Development, no. 101. San Francisco: Jossey-Bass.

3. Rhodes, J. E. (2004). The critical ingredient: Caring youth-staff relationships in after-school settings. In G. G. Noam (ed.), *After-school worlds: Creating space for development and learning* (pp. 145–161). New Directions for Youth Development, no. 101. San Francisco: Jossey-Bass.

4. Miles, M. B., & Huberman, A. M. (1994). *Qualitative data analysis* (2nd ed.). Thousand Oaks, CA: Sage; Ragin, C. C. (2000). *Fuzzy-set social science.* Chicago: University of Chicago Press.

5. We have changed the names of people and programs and insignificant features of the programs we discuss to preserve their anonymity.

6. Eccles, J. S., & Gootman, J. A. (Eds.). (2002). *Community programs to promote youth development.* Washington, DC: National Academy Press.

7. We have also examined another category of dilemmas in which leaders face a tension between supporting youths' ownership of the work and ensuring that their work stays on track. See Larson, R., Hansen, D., & Walker, K. (2005). Everybody's gotta give: Adolescents' development of initiative within a youth program. In J. Mahoney, J. Eccles, & R. Larson (Eds.), *Organized activities as contexts of development* (pp. 159–183). Mahwah, NJ: Erlbaum; Walker, K., & Larson, R. (2004). Life on the ground: Balancing youth ownership with adult input. *Evaluation Exchange, 10*(1), 8.

KATHRIN C. WALKER *is project director for The Youth Development Experience study at the University of Illinois. She is also a research fellow at the University of Minnesota's Center for 4-H and Community Youth Development, where she conducts applied research and evaluation on youth development practice.*

REED W. LARSON *is the Pampered Chef Ltd. Endowed Chair in Family Resilience and a professor in the Department of Human and Community Development at the University of Illinois, Urbana-Champaign. His research deals with adolescent development, particularly in the context of youth development programs.*

Index

Accountability system, 103–104

Adolescents. *See* Youth

Adult wizards: Henry and Iris example of, 86–87; identifying, 53

After-school programs. *See* Youth programs

Akiva, T., 4, 9, 37, 93, 108

Arrieux, D., 4, 9, 93, 108

Art First, 80

Asset-based approach, 80

Bales, S. N., 3, 7, 11, 23, 27

Beth (artistic director), 114–116

Beyer, J., 4, 8, 45, 56

Bigelow, M., 81

Blyth, D. A., 3, 5, 7, 25, 43

Bruininks, R., 12

Choreographer problem case study, 114–115

Communities: assessing development opportunities to identify gaps in, 71; professional learning, 94*fig*, 99–100; types supporting youth development opportunities, 60–61*fig*, 63*t*; What's Up? study implications for, 54–55

Cultures of intentionality, 101–103

Developmental nutrients: caring people, 30; challenging possibilities, 31; constructive places, 30–31; described, 30; developmental meals, 31–32

Developmentally intentional program framework: applied to evaluation of program, 89–91; embracing youth in context of their lives, 81–82; illustrated diagram of, 77*fig*; learning experience model as part of, 82–83, 84*fig*; overview of, 77–79;

youth development ethos element of, 77*fig*, 79–80, 84*fig*, 85–86

Developmentally intentional programs: frontline intentionality of, 94*fig*–95; goodness of fit of, 76; point of service and key developmental experiences, 94*fig*; practical applications of, 89–91; strategies for practice with early adolescents, 83–88; theory of developmental intentionality, 76, 94–95

Developmentally intentional strategies: using activities that draw youth, 88; elements of, 83–85, 84*fig*; ethos transparency, 85–86; relationships as central to, 86–87; Soul Academy use of, 87–88; YouthRESPOND use of, 87

Diet-and-exercise analogy: described, 28–30, 29*t*; developmental nutrients of, 30–32; implications of new paradigm of, 34–41; strengthening developmental muscles, 32–34

Dworkin, J., 4, 8, 45, 56

Ethos. *See* Youth development ethos

Evaluation: developmental intentionality approach to, 89–91; High/Stakes model quality metrics used in, 4, 95–99; implications of new paradigm for, 40–41; Youth Program Quality Assessment (PQA), 98–99. *See also* Youth programs

"Fadumo" (young immigrant woman), 81–82

Farmers' market project, 85–86

Focus groups: formed to explore participation rates, 58–60; Minnesota Commission use of, 18

Notes for Contributors

After reading this issue, you might be inspired to become a contributor. *New Directions for Youth Development: Theory, Practice, and Research* is a quarterly publication focusing on contemporary issues inspiring and challenging the field of youth development. A defining focus of the journal is the relationship among theory, research, and practice. In particular, *NDYD* is dedicated to recognizing resilience as well as risk, and healthy development of our youth as well as the difficulties of adolescence. The journal is intended as a forum for provocative discussion that reaches across the worlds of academia, service, philanthropy, and policy.

In the tradition of the New Directions series, each volume of the journal addresses a single, timely topic, although special issues covering a variety of topics are occasionally commissioned. We welcome submissions of both volume topics and individual articles. All articles should address the implications of theory for practice and research directions, and how these arenas can better inform one another. Articles may focus on any aspect of youth development; all theoretical and methodological orientations are welcome.

If you would like to be an *issue editor*, please submit an outline of no more than four pages that includes a brief description of your proposed topic and its significance along with a brief synopsis of individual articles (including tentative authors and a working title for each chapter).

If you would like to be an *author*, please submit first a draft of an abstract of no more than 1,500 words, including a two-sentence synopsis of the article; send this to the editorial assistant.

For all prospective issue editors or authors:

- Please make sure to keep accessibility in mind, by illustrating theoretical ideas with specific examples and explaining technical terms in nontechnical language. A busy practitioner who may not have an extensive research background should be well served by our work.

- Please keep in mind that references should be limited to twenty-five to thirty. Authors should make use of case examples to illustrate their ideas, rather than citing exhaustive research references. You may want to recommend two or three key articles, books, or Web sites that are influential in the field, to be featured on a resource page. This can be used by readers who want to delve more deeply into a particular topic.
- All reference information should be listed as endnotes, rather than including author names in the body of the article or footnotes at the bottom of the page. The endnotes are in APA style.

Please visit http://www.pearweb.org for more information.

Gil G. Noam
Editor-in-Chief

Back Issue/Subscription Order Form

Copy or detach and send to:
Jossey-Bass, A Wiley Imprint, 989 Market Street, San Francisco, CA 94103-1741

Call or fax toll-free: Phone 888-378-2537 6:30AM – 3PM PST; Fax 888-481-2665

Back issues: Please send me the following issues at $29 each.
(Important: please include series initials and issue number, such as YD100.)

_____

_____

_____

$ _____   Total for single issues

$ _____   Shipping charges: Surface   Domestic   Canadian
                                            First item $5.00 $6.00
                                            Each add'l item $3.00 $1.50
                    For next-day and second-day delivery rates, call the number listed above.

Subscriptions: Please __start __renew my subscription to *New Directions for Youth Development* for the year 2_____ at the following rate:

U.S.	__Individual $80	__Institutional $195
Canada	__Individual $80	__Institutional $235
All others	__Individual $104	__Institutional $269

**For more information about online subscriptions visit
www.interscience.wiley.com**

$ _____   Total single issues and subscriptions (Add appropriate sales tax for your state for single issue orders. No sales tax for U.S. subscriptions. Canadian residents, add GST for subscriptions and single issues.)

__Payment enclosed (U.S. check or money order only)
__VISA __MC __AmEx #_____ Exp. date _____

Signature _____ Day phone _____
__ Bill me (U.S. institutional orders only. Purchase order required.)

Purchase order # _____
                    Federal Tax ID13559302   **GST 89102 8052**

Name _____

Address _____

_____

Phone _____ E-mail _____

For more information about Jossey-Bass, visit our Web site at **www.josseybass.com**

NEW DIRECTIONS FOR YOUTH DEVELOPMENT
IS NOW AVAILABLE ONLINE AT WILEY INTERSCIENCE

What is Wiley InterScience?

Wiley InterScience is the dynamic online content service from John Wiley & Sons delivering the full text of over 300 leading scientific, technical, medical, and professional journals, plus major reference works, the acclaimed *Current Protocols* laboratory manuals, and even the full text of select Wiley print books online.

What are some special features of Wiley InterScience?

Wiley InterScience Alerts is a service that delivers table of contents via e-mail for any journal available on Wiley InterScience as soon as a new issue is published online.

Early View is Wiley's exclusive service presenting individual articles online as soon as they are ready, even before the release of the compiled print issue. These articles are complete, peer-reviewed, and citable.

CrossRef is the innovative multi-publisher reference linking system enabling readers to move seamlessly from a reference in a journal article to the cited publication, typically located on a different server and published by a different publisher.

How can I access Wiley InterScience?

Visit http://www.interscience.wiley.com

Guest Users can browse Wiley InterScience for unrestricted access to journal Tables of Contents and Article Abstracts, or use the powerful search engine.

Registered Users are provided with a *Personal Home Page* to store and manage customized alerts, searches, and links to favorite journals and articles. Additionally, Registered Users can view free Online Sample Issues and preview selected material from major reference works.

Licensed Customers are entitled to access full-text journal articles in PDF, with select journals also offering full-text HTML.

How do I become an Authorized User?

Authorized Users are individuals authorized by a paying Customer to have access to the journals in Wiley InterScience. For example, a university that subscribes to Wiley journals is considered to be the Customer. Faculty, staff, and students authorized by the university to have access to those journals in Wiley InterScience are Authorized Users. Users should contact their Library for information on which Wiley journals they have access to in Wiley InterScience.

ASK YOUR INSTITUTION ABOUT WILEY INTERSCIENCE TODAY!